ALCOHOLISM
Is Neither
Incurable
Nor A Disease!

That's Dr. Claude Steiner's message in his astonishing new best-seller that is giving new hope to problem drinkers and their families. With his new treatment for America's biggest health problem, which the <u>Los Angeles Times</u> has called "amazingly successful," he has cured many problem drinkers who have come to him for help. Now he summarizes his approach and tells how it works:

Why alcoholism is not a disease—and why treating an alcoholic as a "sick" man may do him more harm than good.

How a person chooses a role for himself in early age that may turn him into an alcoholic.

The three distinct types of alcoholics and the different games they play.

How the alcoholic can "unmake" his decision and become truly cured.

GAMES
ALCOHOLICS
PLAY

The Analysis of Life Scripts

Claude Steiner, Ph.D.

BALLANTINE BOOKS • NEW YORK

Library of Congress Catalog Card Number: 74-139254

ISBN 0-345-28470-4

This edition published by arrangement with Grove Press, Inc.

Manufactured in the United States of America

First Ballantine Books Edition: January 1974
Eleventh Printing: March 1982

To my mother, Vally,
Who told me what to do
And my father, Willy,
Who showed me how.

Contents

PART V / TREATMENT OF ALCOHOLISM

Foreword

THE WORD "alcoholic" is only about a hundred years old (1856). It is one of those words ending in "ic" used by clinicians to mean a non-person, like "schizophrenic" and "psychotic." What Dr. Steiner has done here is give back to "alcoholics" their membership cards in the human race.

In general, the less people know about a subject, the longer it takes them to explain it. $E=mC^2$ tells us more about the universe than the whole Alexandrian library did, and a prescription for penicillin is a better solution for pneumonia than all the medieval universities in Europe had to offer. The vast literature on alcoholism is with few exceptions an apology for not being able to do much about it. Two of the most important exceptions are the Twelve Steps of Alcoholics Anonymous, which tell how to do something about it, and this book, which does likewise.

Transactional analysis is a new approach to the problem. Through its consistent theory, it offers a way of organizing observations toward new discoveries and cogent methods of treatment. Dr. Steiner is a pioneer in transactional analysis, a keen and intelligent observer, and an experienced clinician in the field of intoxicants. Even before he reveals his therapeutic strategies, he discusses two sets of observations which are each in themselves important contributions that cannot be overlooked by any serious student. The first is the classification of alcoholics into three different types according to the transactions they engage in. As with all game descriptions, the value of this lies in the recognition factor. Anyone, layman or professional, who has to deal with heavy drinkers personally or clinically, will be able to recognize and distinguish between the three types which Steiner aptly calls Drunk and Proud, Lush, and Wino. It is this very aptness which makes his observations so incisive.

A second important nosological distinction is his discussion of *withdrawal panic* and its psychological basis, as distinct from *withdrawal sickness*. By courageously persisting in his therapeutic efforts beyond the point where most other clinicians retreat, he brings the patient out of what first appears to be a psychosis. To my knowledge, this distinction has never been made before, nor can withdrawal panic be adequately accounted for without a clear understanding of structural analysis. Thus two side issues to the main subject of how to treat alcoholics with psychotherapy become in fact substantial and original discoveries.

Dr. Steiner also introduces the reader, almost in passing, to two other valuable ideas which may be new to those who are not familiar with the recent progress of transactional analysis. These are the Drama Triangle of Karpman, which succinctly portrays the role switches that can take place in the alcoholic games (as well as in other games and in literature and drama), and the theoretical basis for and therapeutic value of protection as described by Crossman.

Thus Steiner first lays a sound theoretical and clinical groundwork before he comes to the core of this book, which tells of the actual therapeutic operations required to break up the alcoholic games and script, operations which, in short, allow the patient to stop drinking. There, with true professionalism, he tells not only what to do, but also what not to do.

Dr. Steiner first summarized these ideas in an article in the *Quarterly Journal of Studies on Alcohol*. There they aroused a rather tempestuous controversy, but most of the criticisms were *ad hominem* rather than *ad rem,* and some of these epithets were directed at myself as well. I can only say that I am proud to be placed beside him in this regard, to have had some hand in the matter, and to have the privilege of writing this Foreword. The indications are that script analysis, properly studied, understood, and applied, is the most effective scientific psychotherapeutic approach to date in the treatment of the alcoholic, and this has been demonstrated by others besides Dr. Steiner. The only way to test this statement is for clinicians to learn the principles of script analysis thoroughly, and apply them conscientiously and powerfully for a year or two in their own practices. They will have to learn the difference between switching roles in the game (Alcoholics Anonymous), "making progress" (other conventional psychotherapies), and breaking up the game itself and the script on which it is based. This book tells them firmly, gently, and benevolently, but with proper clinical objectivity, how to do the last. It also gives the therapist permission to enjoy his work, which is, I think, a unique contribution of the transactional approach, having the added value that it also permits the patient to enjoy his treatment. Cough medicines taste better these days than they used to, and so should psychotherapy.

—Eric Berne, M.D.
1970

Preface

THIS BOOK is primarily an extension of the theory and practice of transactional analysis into the specific area of scripts. In addition, it is hoped that it will provide lay and professional readers with information leading to the understanding and more effective treatment of alcoholism and other addictions. The theoretical background for this book is summarized in Part I. Readers who wish a more thorough background in transactional analysis should read Eric Berne's books, *Transactional Analysis in Psychotherapy* and *Games People Play;* for those especially interested in group treatment, *The Structure and Dynamics of Organizations and Groups* and *Principles of Group Treatment* are also recommended.

Scripts is an area of transactional analysis which has rapidly expanded in the last few years and some of the ideas presented here have been gathered from others. Probably because of my work with alcoholics, in whom scripts are often evident, I was able to organize my ideas into a statement of theory specifically relevant to them, and quite useful in their treatment. Without Dr. Berne's initial thoughts on scripts and his intellectual and moral support, none of the following ideas would have materialized. His previous statements on transactional analysis and scripts are the *sine qua non* of script theory. To Mrs. Patricia Crossman, Dr. John Dusay, Dr. Kenneth Everts, Dr. Martin Groder, Dr. Stephen Karpman, Dr. Ray Poindexter, among others, thanks are due for many of the thoughts presented here and for confirming many of them in their independent professional activities.

Special thanks are due to Dr. George David, Dr. David Geisinger, Dr. Jack Leibman, Mrs. Melissa Nygard, Mr. Neil Ross, and Dr. Robert Zechnick, each of whom painstakingly read the original manuscript and offered suggestions which were used without further credit.

Finally, I wish to thank Mr. Peter Warfield who, with the eye of an informed layman and editor, put the book into its final form.

—Claude Steiner
1971

Introduction

THERE IS powerful and pervasive evidence that alcoholics seem driven, whether sober or drinking, by an inner compulsion for self-destruction. An alcoholic sober for years will commonly return to his previous state of alcoholism regardless of how long he has stayed sober. For Alcoholics Anonymous (AA), this is evidence that alcoholism is incurable, a disease that lurks in the depths of the personality, waiting to spring forth in full strength at the mere consumption of a single drink. Persons who believe in the AA approach feel that "once an alcoholic, always an alcoholic," and recovered alcoholics in AA consider themselves alcoholics regardless of how long they have been sober.

To date, AA has achieved more success in the treatment of alcoholism, when the criterion is sobriety, than any other approach. The group's wisdom about alcoholism is considerable. One of Alcoholics Anonymous' official publications states:[2]*

*This, and subsequent numbered references, refers to the Bibliography at the end of the book.

We alcoholics are men and women who have lost the ability to control our drinking. We know that no real alcoholic *ever* regains control. All of us felt at times that we were regaining control . . . [but] we are convinced to a man that alcoholics of our type are in the grip of a progressive illness. Over any period of time we get worse, never better . . . Physicians who are familiar with alcoholism agree that there is no such thing as making a normal drinker out of an alcoholic.

According to the *Manual on Alcoholism* of the American Medical Association,[29] alcoholism is a

> . . . highly complex illness . . . characterized by preoccupation with alcohol and loss of control over its consumption such as to lead usually to intoxication when drinking is begun; by chronicity; by progression; and by tendency toward relapse.

To say that alcoholism is an illness implies that it is ". . . an interruption or perversion of function of any of the organs, an acquired morbid change in any tissue of an organism, or throughout an organism, with characteristic symptoms caused by specific micro-organismal alterations."[39]

The above definition, however, does not seem to describe a large number of bona fide alcoholics. For instance, can it be said convincingly that a year after his last drink and the day before his next binge a young alcoholic is suffering from an interruption or perversion of the function of an organ or that there is an identifiable morbid change in any of his bodily tissue? Defining alcoholism as an illness implies that its treatment is basically a function of physical medicine. Further, defining it as a progressive or chronic illness implies that its treatment should be approached, as the *Manual* recommends,[29]

> . . . in much the same way as are other chronic and relapsing medical conditions [in which] the aim of treatment is then viewed more as one of control than cure.

The theory of alcoholism as an incurable disease is weakened by evidence, thoroughly documented,[4] that a number of individuals, once unquestioned alcoholics, returned to social drinking without returning to alcoholism. These cases provide evidence that alcoholism is not incurable, always ready to be triggered by the consumption of alcohol.

This book presents a theory about alcoholism in particular, as well as emotional disorders in general, and a method of treatment which follows from this theory. The theory can be called a decision theory rather than a disease theory of alcoholism or emotional disturbance. It is based on the notion that some people make conscious decisions in childhood or early adolescence which influence and make predictable the rest of their lives. Persons whose lives are based on such a decision are said to have a script, and a script may involve life plans such as becoming an alcoholic, committing suicide or homicide, going crazy, or never achieving any success.

Like diseases, scripts have an onset, a course, and an outcome. Because of this similarity, scripts have been mistaken for diseases. However, because scripts are based on consciously willed decisions rather than on morbid tissue changes, they can be revoked or "undecided" by similarly willed decisions. Thus, I believe that a cured alcoholic (though he often does not choose to) will be able to return to social drinking, while the person who returns to uncontrollable drinking after one drink has been essentially unable to dispose of his script.*

Psychoanalytic theories have attempted to show that persistent behavioral disorders such as alcoholism are based on psychic misalignments which persist because they are deeply buried and therefore unconscious. These theories may see the alcoholic as someone with a "passive-aggressive oral character who drinks because of a deep-lying ego deficit"; script theory is more likely

---

*This statement, not novel by any means, may be seen by some, with good reason, as dangerous. A drinking alcoholic may construe it to mean that he can "lick his problem" without quitting. A sober alcoholic may be tempted to "have just one" to see if he *does* have his problem licked. It is hoped, however, that the potential risk to some alcoholics is outweighed by the potential benefit to others, derived from discussing the matter openly and honestly. Also, it is important to distinguish between social drinking and the institutionalized alcoholism that passes as social drinking in our culture.

to see him as someone who decided early in life to lead a self-destructive life based on a game of "Alcoholic" with a certain course and outcome. Yet many persons with a passive-aggressive oral character do not become alcoholics, and in general, psychoanalytic explanations of alcoholism have been regarded with bemused disbelief by most alcoholism workers.

Various psychological theories have attempted to account for alcoholism on the basis of personality traits such as dependency, oral fixation, or latent homosexuality; however, considerable research investigating these theories has failed to show any systematic relationship between these traits and alcoholism.

On the other hand, McCord and McCord found that while "alcoholics were, in childhood, not plagued by inferiority feelings, oral tendencies or homosexual leanings more than 'normal' men,"[28] there did seem to be a prevalence of certain situations that characterized the childhood homes of future alcoholics. Script theory agrees with this and goes on to say that, for the alcoholic, it is these situations, according to script theory, that lead to conscious decisions that eventually lead to an alcoholic life course.

The same statement can be made about other kinds of disturbances which are parts of life scripts, such as suicide, homosexuality, drug addiction, or "mental illnesses" such as schizophrenia.

Considering alcoholism a script rather than an incurable disease makes possible a more thorough understanding and a treatment approach which enables a competent practitioner to cure the alcoholic so that he may "close down the show and put a new one on the road." Questioning the assumption that alcoholism is incurable also generates positive expectancy and hope, whose importance Frank[18] and Goldstein[22] have amply documented. From their studies, it is clear that an assumption of chronicity and illness on the part of workers will have the effect of generating chronicity and illness in the patient, while an assumption of curability will tend to generate cures. Thus, considering alcoholism a chronic illness, as many who work with alcoholics do, may be potentially harmful to, and may in fact promote illness and chronicity in, large numbers of alcoholics. On the other hand, the assumption that alcoholism and other psychiatric disturbances are curable because they are based on a reversible decision, will bring to bear the potent effect of positive expectancy on their treatment.

The following pages describe the various aspects and stages of life scripts and their treatment. Examples from case histories of alcoholics will be used throughout, although not exclusively. Sections on the alcoholic game and the treatment of alcoholics are included.

Part I

Transactional Theory of Personality

CHAPTER ONE

Structural and Transactional Analysis

As A theory of personality, Eric Berne's transactional analysis is a branch, rather close to the roots, on the tree of psychoanalytic personality theory. Transactional analysis is essentially sympathetic to psychoanalytic concepts of personality. As a theory and method of treatment, however, it differs from psychoanalytic theory in a number of significant ways which will be elaborated in the section on treatment.

The building blocks of the theory of transactional analysis (TA) are three observable forms of ego function: the Parent, the Adult, and the Child. They may seem to resemble three basic psychoanalytic concepts—the supergo, the ego and the id—but they are, in fact, quite different.

The Parent, Adult, and Child differ from the superego, ego, and id because they are all manifestations of the ego. Thus, they represent visible behavior rather than hypothetical constructs. When a person is in one of the three ego states, for instance the Child, the observer is able to see and hear the Child, while no one has ever seen the id or superego. TA focuses on the ego

3

and on consciousness because these concepts explain and predict behavior better than the usual psycho-analytic concepts.

STRUCTURAL ANALYSIS

A person operates in one of three distinct ego states at any one time. These ego states are distinguishable by skeletal-muscular variables and the content of verbal utterances. Certain gestures, postures, mannerisms, facial expressions, and intonations, as well as certain words, are typically associated with one of the three ego states. In examining his own behavior, an observer also has information about his emotional state and thoughts which are part of the ego state being observed. Diagnosis of ego states is made by observing the visible and audible characteristics of a person's appearance or ego.

THE CHILD

The Child ego state is essentially preserved in its entirety from childhood. When a person is functioning in this ego mode, he behaves as he did when he was a little boy or a little girl. Current thinking holds that the Child is never more than about seven years old and may be as young as one hour or one day. When a person is in the Child ego state, he sits, stands, walks, and speaks as he did when he was, say, three years old. This child-like behavior is accompanied by the corresponding perceptions, thoughts, and feelings of a three-year-old.[41]

The Child ego state tends to be fleeting in grownups because of a general societal injunction against "childish behavior." However, Child ego states can be observed in situations which are structured to permit childlike behavior, such as sports events, parties, and church revivals. A good place to view the Child ego state in grownups is at a football game. Here, childlike expressions of joy, anger, rage, and delight can be observed, and it is easy to see how, aside from bone size and secondary sexual characteristics, a man jumping for joy when his team scores is indistinguishable from a five-year-old boy. The similarity goes further than the observable behavior since the man is not only acting as a boy, but feeling, seeing, and thinking as a boy.

In the Child ego state, a person tends to use short words and expletives like "golly," "gee," and "nice," delivered in a high-pitched voice. He adopts stances characteristic of children: a downward tilt of the head, upturned eyes, feet apart or pigeon-toed. When sitting, the person may balance on the edge of the chair, fidgeting, rocking, or slouching. Jumping, clapping, laughing expansively, or crying are all part of the repertoire of the Child ego state.

Aside from situations which permit childlike behavior, the Child can be observed in a fixated form in schizophrenics and in such persons as comedians, whose profession requires them to appear habitually in a Child ego state, and in female sex symbols like Marilyn Monroe. Of course, the Child ego state is readily observable in children.

A Child ego state much younger than a year is rarely observed, since persons who habitually express this ego state are usually severely disturbed. However, this type of a very young Child appears in normal persons under circumstances of severe stress, or when great pain or joy is felt.

The value of the Child should not be underestimated. It is said to be the best part of a person and the only part that can really enjoy itself. It is the source of spontaneity, creative change, and is the mainspring of joy.

THE ADULT

The Adult ego state is essentially a computer, an impassionate organ of the personality, which gathers and processes data for the purpose of making predictions. The Adult gathers data about the world through the senses, processes them according to a logical program, and makes predictions when necessary. Its perception is diagrammatic. While the Child perceives in color, in space, and from one point of view at a time, the Adult may perceive in black and white, often in two dimensions, and from several points of view at the same time. In the Adult ego state, a person is isolated from his own affective and other internal processes, a condition indispensable for the proper observation and prediction of reality. Thus, in the Adult ego state the person "has no feelings," even though he may be able to appraise his Child or Parent feelings. Often the rational Parent ego state is confused with the Adult ego state. However, the Adult is not only rational but is also without emotion.

According to Piaget's detailed discussion of "formal operations," the Adult grows gradually during childhood.[35] This development proceeds as a consequence of the interaction between the person and the external world.

The Parent

The Parent is essentially made up of behavior copied from parents or authority figures. It is taken whole, as perceived at an early age, without modification. A person in the Parent ego state is a play-back of a video tape recording of his parent or whoever was or is *in loco parentis.*

Thus, the Parent ego state is essentially nonperceptive and noncognitive. It is simply a constant and sometimes arbitrary basis for decisions, the repository of traditions and values, and it is vital to the survival of children and civilization. It operates validly when adequate information for an Adult decision is not available, but in certain people, it operates in spite of adequate Adult information.

The Parent, while taken whole from others, is not a fixated ego state since it can change over time. Thus, a person's experiences can add to or subtract from his Parent's repertoire of behavior. For instance, rearing a firstborn child will greatly increase the range of responses of the Parent. In general, the Parent ego state seems to change throughout life, from adolescence to old age, as the person encounters new situations that demand parental behavior, and as the person finds authority figures from whom examples for such behavior are adopted.

Structural analysis is organized around the fundamental concepts of these ego states. Some further concepts in structural analysis will be advanced. Ego states operate one at a time, that is, a person is always in one and only one of the three ego states. This ego state is called the executive, or is said to have executive power. While one ego state has the executive power, the person may be aware of literally standing beside himself, observing his own behavior. The feeling that the "self" is not the ego state in the executive usually occurs when the Child or Parent has executive power, while the "real self," perhaps the Adult, observes without being able to behave. Thus, while only one ego state is cathected, that is, imbued with the energy necessary to activate muscular complexes involved in behavior, it is possible for another ego state to be sufficiently cathected to become conscious to the person, even though it is unable to activate the musculature.

Since a person can operate in one ego state while another state observes, internal dialogues between these ego states become possible. For example, after a few drinks at a party, a man may be swept by the music into an expansive, childlike dance. His Child is now in the executive while the Parent observes his gyrations and mutters something like, "You're making a fool of yourself, Charlie," or, "This is all very well, but what about your slipped disk?" Often this comment by the nonexecutive ego state decathects the Child and transfers the executive to the Parent, in which case Charlie will stop dancing, perhaps blush, and retire to his seat where the situation will be reversed and Charlie, now in the Parent ego state, will look disapprovingly at other dancers. Becoming aware of the conversations that occur between the executive and the observing state is a very important step in therapy, as has been pointed out elsewhere by Ellis.[13]

It is somewhat difficult to diagnose ego states because people tend to masquerade their Child and Parent as Adult ego states. Opinionated and judgmental attitudes are often couched in rational language. The Parent, masquerading as an Adult, may express very logical points of view, but the Parental nature is revealed by the emphasis or the unspoken but clear attempt to impose the points of view on others. From his Adult ego state, a husband might ask his wife, "Why isn't dinner ready?" From his Parent masquerading as an Adult, he may ask the identical question. The difference, however, is that in the former case, the husband is simply asking a question, while in the latter he is attempting to pressure and blame the wife for being lazy and disorganized.

Sometimes two sets of muscles may seem to be powered by two separate ego states at the same time. For instance, a lecturer's voice and facial muscles may indicate an Adult ego state, while an impatient toss of the hand reveals a Parent ego state. In such cases, it is likely that the behavior is Parent in Adult disguise and therefore Parent, or that Parent and Adult are alternating rapidly.

Alternation between ego states depends on the permeability of the ego state boundaries. Permeability is an important variable in psychotherapy. Low permeability leads to exclusion of appropriate ego states. Exclusions of the Parent, Adult, and Child ego states are all pathological since they preclude the use of ego states that, in a given situation, may be more adaptive than the excluding ego state.

For example, at a party the excluding adult is less adaptive than the Child. The purpose of the party is to have fun, which the Child can do, but the Adult, analyzing and computing data dispassionately, would deter the party's purpose. A father with an excluding Adult prevents the more adaptive Parent from properly raising his children. For example, when Johnny asks his father, "Daddy, why do I have to go to bed?" the Adult response would be a lecture about the physiology, psychology, and sociology of sleep. The more adaptive Parent would simply say, "The reason you have to go to sleep is because I said so," or, "Because it's bedtime," an answer which is much more appropriate to the situation.

On the other hand, extreme permeability is another form of pathology often manifested by the inability to remain in the Adult ego state for a sufficient period of time.

Every ego state, being a substructure of the ego, is, in its own way, an adaptive "organ," having as its function adaptation to the demands of reality. How the ego as a whole functions adaptively has been elucidated by Hartman;[25] all three ego states share in this function, each one specially suited for specific situations. It might be said that the Parent is ideally suited where control is necessary—control of children, of unknown situations, of fears, of unwanted expression of people, and of the Child. The Adult is suited to situations in which accurate prediction is necessary. The Child is ideally suited where creation is desired—creation of new ideas, procreation, creation of new experiences, recreation, and so on.

One more concept of great importance is contamination. This phenomenon is characterized by an Adult ego state holding as fact certain ideas stemming from the Parent or the Child. For instance, a Parental idea such as "masturbation leads to insanity" or "women are passive creatures" could be part of a person's Adult ego state. Or, the Adult might be contaminated by an idea such as "grownups can't be trusted." Decontamination of the Adult is an early therapeutic requirement in treat-

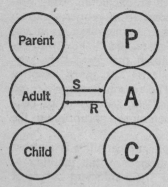

A. Complementary Transaction
Stimulus (S): How much is 3 x 5?
Response (R): Fifteen.

B. Crossed Transaction
S: How much is 3 x 5?
R: I hate math!

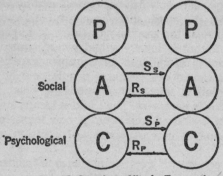

C. Complex or Ulterior Transaction
S social: Let's work late, Miss Smith.
S psychological: Let's have a drink, Sally.

Figure 1

ment and is accomplished through an accurately timed confrontation by the therapist's Adult with the inaccuracy of the ideas which are causing the contamination.

A very successful technique to decontaminate ego states is having the person alternately speak first for one, then another, of his ego states. This technique, originated in psychodrama and later adapted by Gestalt therapy, is a very convincing demonstration of the reality of ego states. A person who feels guilty because of masturbation could be asked to speak from his Parent about the evils of masturbation, from his Child about the guilt and fears of insanity due to his masturbation, and from his Adult about the well-known fact that masturbation is harmless and normal. Verbalizing these different points of view tends to separate the two ego states, a process which facilitates decontamination of the Adult.

Thus, the theory of TA is based on variables observable and verifiable by patients as well as therapists or theorists. The wish to include the patient in the understanding, observation, and verification of behavior theories generates the extensive use of colloquialisms, and the insistence that most of the relevant variables in treatment are conscious and therefore available to the patient himself by simple attention to certain areas of his behavior.

TRANSACTIONAL ANALYSIS

Just as the ego state is the unit of structural analysis, so the transaction is the unit of transactional analysis. The theory holds that a person's behavior is best understood if examined in terms of ego states, and that the behavior between two or more persons is best understood if examined in terms of transactions. A transaction consists of a stimulus and a response between two specific ego states. In a simple transaction, only two ego states operate. One example is a transaction between two Adult ego states: "How much is five times seven?" "Thirty-five." All other combinations of ego states may occur in a transaction. Transactions follow one another smoothly as long as the stimulus and response are parallel or complementary (Figure 1).

In any series of transactions, communication proceeds if the response to a previous stimulus is addressed to the ego state that was the source of the stimulus and is emitted from the ego state to which that source addressed itself. Any other response creates a crossed transaction and interrupts communication. In Figure 1, transaction A is complementary and will lead to further communication, while transaction B is crossed and will break off communication. Crossed transactions not only account for the interruption of communication but also are an essential part of games.

In addition to simple and crossed transactions, another very important form is the complex, ulterior transaction. It operates on two levels: social and psychological. In Figure 1, transaction C is between A and A: "Let's work late on these accounts, Miss Smith, we'll catch dinner on the way to the office"; and between C and C: "Let's have dinner and drinks together, Sally, and maybe we'll get some work done later." In an ulterior transaction, the social level usually covers the real (psychological) meaning of the transaction; thus interpersonal behavior is not understandable until the ulterior level and ego states involved are understood.

GAMES

A game is a behavioral sequence which 1) is an orderly series of transactions with a beginning and an end; 2) contains an ulterior motive, that is, a psychological level different from the social level; and 3) results in a payoff for both players.

The motivation for playing games comes from their

payoff. To use an analogy, structural analysis describes the relevant parts of the personality, just as a parts list describes the parts of an engine. Transactional analysis describes the way in which the parts interact, just as a cutaway engine shows how the engine parts relate to each other. But to understand *why* people transact with each other at all, some driving force has to be postulated and this explanation is found in the motivational concepts of *stimulus hunger, structure hunger,* and *position hunger.* Games provide satisfaction for all three of these hungers and this satisfaction is referred to as the advantage, or payoff, of the game.

STIMULUS HUNGER

Considerable research indicates that stimulation is one of the primary needs of higher organisms. Based on these findings and on clinical evidence, Berne evolved the concepts of stimulus hunger and stroking.[8]

A stroke is a special form of stimulation one person gives to another. Because strokes are essential to a person's survival, the exchange of strokes is one of the most important activities people engage in. Strokes can vary from actual physical stroking to praise, or just recognition. To be effective, a stroke must be suited to its recipient. For example, Spitz has shown that a very young child needs actual physical stroking.[38] On the other hand, adults may require only occasional, symbolic strokes such as praise, or an expression of appreciation.

Stimulus hunger is satisfied by stroking or recognition. Stroking is a more basic need than recognition and it is said that a person needs stroking "lest his spinal cord shrivel up." Usually, the need for actual physical stroking is eventually largely replaced with symbolic stroking or recognition. Thus the average adult can satisfy his hunger for stroking through, among other things, a ritual which is essentially an exchange of recognition strokes. For example, the following is a six-stroke ritual:

A: Hi.
B: Hi.
A: How are you?
B: Fine, and you?
A: Fine. Well, see you.
B: Yeah, see you around.

A game is transactionally more complex than the above ritual but it is still an exchange of strokes. It might be noted in passing that "Go to hell!" is as much a stroke as "Hi" and people will settle for the former form when they cannot obtain the latter.

Certain persons are unable to accept overt or direct recognition, requiring more disguised forms instead. Such an example is the woman who rejects all admiration of her looks, interpreting them as sexual advances, but accepts compliments about her sewing ability. People who cannot obtain or accept direct recognition for one reason or another will tend to obtain it by playing games which are a rich source of strokes.

STRUCTURE HUNGER

The satisfaction of structure hunger is the social advantage of the game. Structure hunger is the need to establish a social matrix within which the person can transact with others. To satisfy structure hunger, the individual seeks social situations within which time is structured, or organized, for the purpose of obtaining strokes. This need for time structure is an elaboration of stimulus hunger, and therefore just a more complex form of that basic need. A game structures time in many ways. For instance, a game of "If It Weren't For You" (IWFY) provides for considerable time structure with its endless face-to-face recriminations. It provides for additional time structure in that it makes possible the pastime* of "If It Weren't For Him (Her)," played

---

*A pastime is a series of simple, complementary transactions relating to a single subject matter.

with neighbors and relatives, and sometimes, "If It Weren't For Them," played at bars and bridge clubs.

POSITION HUNGER

The satisfaction of position hunger is the existential advantage of the game. Position hunger is the need to vindicate certain basic, life-long, existential positions. These existential positions, colloquially known as the patient's "racket," can be illustrated with a sentence, such as "I am no good," "They are no good," or "Nobody is any good." They are satisfied by internal transactions which take place in the mind of the player between himself and another person, usually a parent. Position hunger is satisfied by stroking or recognition received internally, from the Parent.

Thus, after a game of "Rapo,"* the players go home and White may say to herself, "That proves men are beasts; are you happy, Dad?" and her Parent will answer, "That's my good little girl." This transaction has stroking value, and at the same time reinforces the existential position of the player. As will be elaborated later, every game has the added effect of advancing the *script,* or life plan of the person.

A game provides strokes for the player, without the threat of intimacy. The theory postulates that two or more persons can only structure time together with work, rituals, pastimes, games, withdrawal, or intimacy. Intimacy, which is a social situation free of these other time-structuring elements, is one in which strokes are given directly, and therefore most powerfully. Intimacy can be a threat to the person because it goes counter to Parental prohibitions about the exchange of strokes. Thus, a game is a carefully balanced procedure to procure strokes that are safe from Parental criticism.

It should be noted that strokes can be obtained without resorting to games, which are basically subterfuges, and that games are learned in childhood from parents as

*See "Rapo," p. 17.

a preferred method of obtaining stimulation. Thus, a person giving up a game has to develop an alternate way of obtaining strokes and structuring time, and until he does he will be subject to despair resembling marasmus in children who do not receive enough stroking.

Two games will be described in detail. The first is a "soft" game called "Why Don't You—Yes But," and the second is a "medium hard" version (second-degree) of "Rapo." The softness or hardness of a game refers to the intensity with which it is played and the morbidity of its effects. First degree is the "soft" version, and third degree the "hard" version of a game.

"Why Don't You—Yes But" (YDYB) is a common game played wherever people gather in groups, and generally proceeds as follows:

Black and White are mothers of grade-school children.
White: I sure would like to come to the PTA meeting but I can't get a baby sitter. What should I do?
Black: Why don't you call Mary? She'd be glad to sit for you.
White: She is a darling girl, but she is too young.
Black: Why don't you call the baby-sitting service? They have experienced ladies.
White: Yes, but some of those old ladies look like they might be too strict.
Black: Why don't you bring the kids along to the meeting?
White: Yes, but I would be embarrassed to be the only one to come with her children.
Finally, after several such transactions there is silence, perhaps followed by a statement by another person, such as:
Green: It sure is hard to get around when you have kids.

YDYB, first analyzed by Berne, fulfills the three parts of the definition of a game. It is a series of transactions beginning with a question and ending with an irritated silence. It contains an ulterior motive because, at the social level, it is a series of Adult questions and Adult answers, whereas at the psychological level it is a series of questions by a demanding, reluctant Child unable to solve a problem and a series of answers by an increasingly irritated Parent anxious to help in a quandary.

Finally, the payoff of the game is as follows: It is a rich source of strokes as it provides a readily usable form of time structure wherever people congregate and reinforces an existential position. The position, in this case, is exemplified by Green's statement, "It sure is hard to get around when you have kids." For White, the game proves that parents are no good and always want to dominate you, and at the same time proves that children are no good and prevent you from doing things. For Black, the game proves that children, or grownups who behave like children, are ungrateful and unwilling to cooperate. For both Black and White, the existential advantage fits into their script. Both White and Black come away from the game feeling angry or depressed according to what their favorite feeling racket is. After a long enough succession of YDYB and similar games, both White and Black may feel justified in getting a divorce, attempting suicide, or simply giving up.

"Rapo." This game is played by a more special type of personality; while YDYB can be played by almost anyone, the psychological content of "Rapo" attracts fewer persons. It is a sexual game, so it requires a man and a woman, although it may be played between homosexuals as well. It proceeds typically, as follows:

At a party, after considerable flirtation, White and Black find themselves in the bedroom with Black reading from the *Kama Sutra*. Aroused by the inviting situation, Black makes an advance and attempts to kiss White. White rebuffs Black and leaves abruptly.

Again we have a series of transactions, beginning with a sexual invitation and ending with a sexual rebuff. On the social level, the game looks like a straightforward flirtation ended by Black's breach of etiquette, rightfully rebuffed by White. On the psychological level, between Child and Child, White has first enticed and then humiliated Black.

The payoff, again, consists of strokes, a way to structure time, and existentially, a ratification of the position "Women (men) are no good," followed by feelings of anger or depression, according to preference. Again the script is advanced since enough episodes of this game may justify a murder, rape, suicide, or depression for the players.

Related to the payoff in games is the concept colloquially called "trading stamps." Trading stamps, or enduring, non-genuine feelings such as anger, depression, low self-esteem, sadness, etc.,* are "collected" and saved up by persons who play games so that when enough are accumulated they can be traded in for a "free" blow-up, drunken binge, suicide attempt, or some other script milestone.

A racket previously defined as the person's existential position finds expression through the activity of collecting trading stamps. The person, for instance, whose existential position is "I'm no good" can continually promote this position by the collection of low self-esteem stamps (gray stamps), while the person whose position is "You're no good" can do the same through the collection of anger stamps (red stamps).

---

*The only enduring feelings that are considered genuine are joy and despair due to a loss. Sudden anger may be genuine, but not if it endures beyond the events that cause the anger.

CHAPTER TWO

Second Order Structural Analysis

SCRIPT ANALYSIS requires an understanding of second order structural analysis, or the analysis of the structure of the Child.

Let us consider a five-year-old child, Mary (Figure 2A), who is capable of operating in three ego states. In her Parent ego state (P_1) she scolds and cuddles her little brother as she sees her mother do; in her Adult ego state (A_1), the Professor, she asks difficult questions ("What is sex, Daddy?" "What is blood for?"); in her Child ego state (C_1) she behaves as she did when she was two years old—she talks babytalk, throws a tantrum, or rolls around on the floor.

Thirty years later, Mary (Figure 2B) is still capable of behaving in three separate ego states. The Parent (P_2) disciplines her five-year-old daughter or nurses her newborn baby; her Adult (A_2) knows how to cook, perform an appendectomy, and make accurate predictions about events and people; her Child (C_2) is identical with the five-year-old Mary described above. Of the three modes of the Child in the thirty-five-year-old Mary, one of them is most likely to be apparent; Mary's per-

19

sonality, as it is known to others, will depend on which of the three possible ego states is usually cathected.

If her Child (C_2) is primarily P_1, she is likely to have a script which is the result of her parents' behavior when Mary was, say, five years old. She will behave in ways exemplified and forced on her by her parents. This Child ego state, P_1 in C_2, has also been called the Adapted Child because, while still a Child ego state, it is molded to parental demands. In the case of persons with self-destructive scripts it is also called "the electrode" because of the electrifying manner in which it seems to control the person's mental life and behavior. In these cases P_1 in C_2 is also called the "witch mother" or "orgre" because it seems to have supernatural qualities similar to the witches and ogres in fairy tales.

If Mary's Child (C_2) behaves mostly as A_1, the Professor, she will be inquisitive and lively ("bright-eyed and bushy tailed"), as contrasted to the more emotive, powerful, perhaps overwhelming behavior of C_1 which is called the Natural Child, or the "prince" or "princess."

When in the Natural Child ego state (C_1) the individual is "turned on" or in a "peak experience." Some people's Child is exclusively the Natural Child; but as societal strictures against this form of behavior are strong, the Child of very few people operates at that level. The acute psychotic state in which a confused Natural Child takes over completely is in essence the breakthrough of the Natural Child after a period of domination by the Parent.

It is important to distinguish, in thirty-five-year-old Mary, the Parent (P_2) from the Parent in the Child (P_1 in C_2). Both ego states are superficially similar in that they both involve certain behavior which is parental, such as finger wagging and certain words such as "ought," "should," etc. Upon close examination, however, the differences become clear. P_1 in C_2 is a little girl acting like mother while P_2 *is* the mother. P_1 in C_2

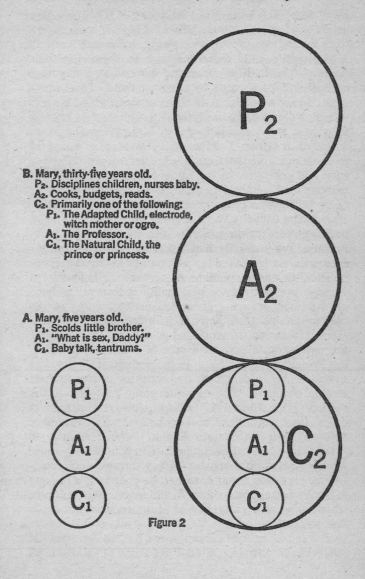

B. Mary, thirty-five years old.
 P_2. Disciplines children, nurses baby.
 A_2. Cooks, budgets, reads.
 C_2. Primarily one of the following:
  P_1. The Adapted Child, electrode,
   witch mother or ogre.
  A_1. The Professor.
  C_1. The Natural Child, the
   prince or princess.

A. Mary, five years old.
 P_1. Scolds little brother.
 A_1. "What is sex, Daddy?"
 C_1. Baby talk, tantrums.

Figure 2

wants to be like mother and imitates her ("Johnny, you better be good"), all the while checking for reassurance from the parents ("How am I doing, Mommy?").

The fundamental difference between them is in their potency. The P_1 in C_2 is neither convincing nor potent except perhaps as seen by a young child. The Parent (P_2), on the other hand, is both convincing and potent. When challenged, P_1 in C_2 tends to collapse and revert to what it truly is, a little girl or boy pretending to be a mother or father. The Parent, however, does not yield to challenge and therefore is experienced by others as solid and powerful. Its solidity is based on the fact that persons in the Parent ego state perceive themselves as O.K., fully grown human beings with physical attributes, such as the capacity to bear children, to nurture them, and to protect them physically—attributes that are lacking in a five-year-old child behaving like a mother or father.

The Adult in the Child (A_1) is called the Professor because this part of the personality is thought to have an extremely accurate grasp and understanding of the major variables that enter into interpersonal relationships. This grasp is manifested in the capacity to detect the psychological, covert aspect of relationships. Thus the Professor, or the Adult in the youngster, is tuned in to and is able to detect the real meaning of transactions and is therefore able to understand that which the second order Adult (A_2) misses. However, in matters other than psychological transactions, the Professor operates with limited information. A good analogy to clarify this point can be found in a very shrewd peasant who is able to hold his own in any interpersonal situation in his home town, but when he goes to the big city is simply not able to cope with the much more complex situation requiring a great deal of information not available to him.

The Parent in the Child (P_1) is a fixated ego state not amenable to change. Unlike the Parent (P_2) which, as was explained previously, changes over time, P_1 in C_2 can only be affected by decommissioning it. In treatment, this is referred to as "showing father or mother to the door," and implies that the P_1 in C_2 is decathected and not allowed to exert its influence on the rest of the personality.

Part II

Scripts

CHAPTER THREE

Oedipus Revisited

A SCRIPT is essentially the blueprint for a life course. Like theatrical tragedy, the alcoholic script follows the Aristotelian principles of dramaturgy. According to Aristotle, the plot of a good tragedy contains three parts: prologue, climax, and catastrophe. These three stages of the script correspond to the onset, course, and outcome of diseases. Because of this, the characterization of life courses as illnesses has been possible. The prologue in the alcoholic's life is his childhood, and its protagonists are his two parents. The climax is the period in adulthood during which the alcoholic struggles against the script and appears to be escaping his destiny or catastrophe. The climax is essentially a highly unstable situation. It represents the battle between two forces: the script or self-destructive tendency, and the wish to avoid the catastrophe. The climax suddenly yields to the catastrophe when the person relaxes his battle against the script and allows his destiny to take its course.

In addition to this tripartite requirement for the plot of good tragic drama, Aristotle postulates that the tragic

27

hero is a good man with but one basic flaw or error (*hamartia*).[3] Because persons with tragic scripts also seem to suffer from a basic flaw, their scripts are referred to as "hamartic." Alcoholism is only one of the situations that may satisfy hamartic script requirements. Similar self-destructive behavior like drug addiction, obesity, excessive smoking, suicide, "mental illness," and certain self-destructive sexual deviations may all be part of hamartic scripts as well.

Once the similarity between modern life courses and ancient Greek tragedies is recognized, it is possible to better understand man's afflictions by looking into the thoughts which Aristotle and subsequently Freud had on the subject of tragedy.

In all tragic scripts, and in the *Oedipus Rex* cycle in particular, a hero, well known to all, does something that is known to all beforehand, and does it in a relentless, predictable, fatal way. From the outset, the audience knows of the hero's eventual demise or change of fortune, yet is fascinated not only by the similarity between the events occurring in the tragedy and the events in their own lives, but also by the manner in which the script unfolds in a predictable and relentless manner.

The tragic deed and outcome of Sophocles' Oedipus are not only known before viewing by most audiences, but within the tragedy itself are known to three different oracles who all concur that Oedipus will commit patricide and incest. In addition, Tiresias predicts the events of the play when he says: "But it will be shown that [Laius' murderer] is a Theban/ A revelation that will fail to please a blind man/ Who has his eyes now; a penniless man who is rich now."[37] All predictions of the tragedy come true, and inevitably adds to the fascination of the Oedipus cycle.

In scripts, too, a prediction is made of what is to come. For instance, a forty-five-year-old alcoholic patient reported to me that, as far as he was concerned, his alcoholism was the result of a prediction made fifteen years before by a Siamese sage. He explained that as a young man on leave from his aircraft carrier, he had visited Siam and gone to a soothsayer. The old man predicted, after some conversation with him, that the patient would die an alcoholic. Fifteen years later he found himself irresistibly drawn to alcohol and fearing that he would indeed die an alcoholic. He realized (his Adult knew) that it does not make sense to believe his alcoholism was caused by the old man's prediction, but he nevertheless felt (his Child believed) that it was and that he was powerless in the face of the apparently inevitable outcome. This man was like the spectator of a tragedy on the stage. For him, the events of his life unfolded according to the prophesies of an oracle, just as Oedipus unbelievingly saw Tiresias' prediction come to pass.

A script is a life plan, containing within its lines what of significance will happen to the person; a plan not decided upon by gods, but finding its origin early in life, in a premature decision by the youngster. It could be speculated that, with the above alcoholic, the wise old man was able to see the patient's self-destructive bent, which was later to unfold; it is common for persons like clinic intake workers, who interview large numbers of people, to see self-destructive tendencies long before the protagonist himself recognizes them. The script guides the person's behavior from late childhood throughout life, determining its general but most basic outlines, and the trained observer is often able to detect and predict the course of a person's life quite accurately.

This is hardly surprising to anyone who has heard the life plans made by young children who later become engineers, lawyers, or doctors. In the area of successful achievement, it is understood that the young child often makes a decision about his life career, but the statement is much more startling when used without prejudice on all life careers, the alcoholic and the suicidal as well as the engineer and the lawyer.

As mentioned above, Aristotle describes the tragic hero not as a man whose misfortune is brought upon him by vice or depravity, but one whose inner flaw causes him to commit a great error of judgment. According to Aristotle, the poet writing a true tragedy must write about situations where the tragic deed is done or mediated by brother on brother, by son on father, by mother on son, or son on mother, because only these situations will arouse the audience to true pity or fear.

Judging from Freud's comments in *The Interpretation of Dreams*,[20] until his time *Oedipus Rex* was seen as a tragedy of destiny, one ". . . whose tragic effect is said to lie in the contrast between the supreme will of the gods and the vain attempts of mankind to escape the evils that threaten them." This view has its origin in Aristotle's *Poetics*[3] and Freud rejected this notion of destiny versus man in favor of the hypothesis that the incestuous content of the tragedy moves the audience rather than the tragedy-of-destiny aspect.

Freud postulated that the frequent wish of his male patients to kill their fathers and bed down with their mothers had its counterpart in the Oedipus tale.[20] According to Freud, the Oedipus cycle is a source of vicarious fear and pity because it reflects a basic household drama experienced by all children who grow up with their parents.

However, script theory, with due regard to the importance of the Oedipus complex, focuses rather on the fated, predicted, ongoing destiny-aspect of *Oedipus Rex*. It bids the reader observe and reconsider the theory rejected by Freud that the message spectators glean from the tragedy and the aspect which deeply moves them is the realization of, and submission to, divine will and the realization of their own impotence in the face of fate.

The Child in the spectator is moved both by the similarity of the Oedipus tragedy and the events in his own household, and by the manner in which certain

specified destinies unfold in wh
manner. The psychologist as a s
Greek tragedies and of present-d
learns, or should learn, that human
affected by and submissive to the will
divinities of their household—their paren
they feel essentially impotent against their in

ts

at seems an irrevocable
ectator, both of the
ay human tragedy,
eings are deeply
of the specific
s—and that
unctions.

31

f Children

THE SCRIPT, then, is based on a decision made by
the Adult in the young person who, with all of the information at his disposal at the time, decides that a
certain position and life course are a reasonable solution
to the existential predicament in which he finds himself.
His predicament comes from the conflict between his
own autonomous tendencies and the injunctions received from his primary family group.

The most important influence or pressure impinging
upon the youngster originates from the parental Child.
That is, the Child ego states in the parent of the person
are the determining factors in the formation of scripts.

WITCHES, OGRES, AND CURSES

The world of fairy tales provides the student of human nature with useful clues to personality. Fairy tales
tend to include a witch or an ogre, a fact which, just as
is the case with the Oedipus tragedy, is an intuitive
bull's-eye. The household parallel corresponding to
witches and ogres is, of course, mothers and fathers.

That is, some children are affected by their mothers or fathers as if by witches or ogres, and this view of them can become an important factor in the make-up of their personality.

Every person has three ego states, and in trying to understand that person, the three ego states of both his mother and father have to be understood as well (Figure 3). For persons with self-destructive scripts, the Child ego state in father or mother (C_F or C_M) has essentially all the features of an ogre or witch. This ogre or witch, generally known as the parent's "crazy Child," has its most profound influence on the offspring. In these cases, the young three- or four-year-old is under the unquestioned and unquestionable rule of a confused, scared, often wanton, and always irrational Child.

According to Crossman,[11] the child in a normal household is essentially nurtured, protected, and raised by the Parent ego state of his parents, with their Adult and Child playing lesser roles. These lesser roles, however, are not unimportant since the Adult in the parent teaches the offspring the rules of logic, and the Child ego state of the parent plays an extremely important part in exciting and encouraging the Natural Child in the offspring. Nevertheless, the Parent ego state of the parents is the one that carries the burden of child-rearing and neither the Child nor the Adult is allowed to take full command in such normal situations.

In a "hamartia-genic" household, however, it is not the Parent of father or mother (P_F or P_M) who is in charge of bringing up the offspring, but a pseudo-Parent which is in reality a Child ego state (C_F or C_M). This Child ego state is basically incapable of performing the necessary functions of a father or mother, and where the Child becomes a pseudo-Parent, the offspring generally develop scripts.

The child's predicament in a hamartia-genic household is illustrated in Figure 3B. In this example, the father of a four-year-old, who later became Little

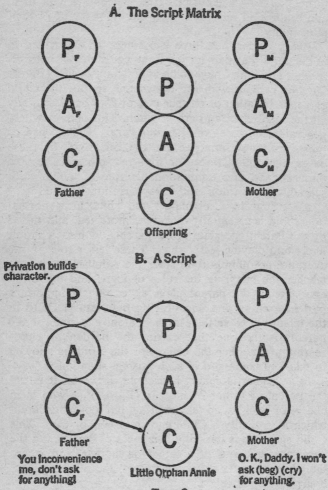

A. The Script Matrix

Father — P_F, A_F, C_F

Offspring — P, A, C

Mother — P_M, A_M, C_M

B. A Script

Privation builds character.

Father — P, A, C_F

You inconvenience me, don't ask for anything!

Little Orphan Annie

Mother — P, A, C

O. K., Daddy. I won't ask (beg) (cry) for anything.

Figure 3

Orphan Annie, allowed his own Child (C_F) to become a pseudo-Parent. This man's Child was annoyed by his daughter's needs. He also believed that the best way to build character in a little girl and to avoid spoiling her was to deny her everything she wanted, and to give her something else in its place. If the little girl wanted a teddy bear for Christmas and he knew about it, he would get her an equally lovely toy that she didn't want, believing that this would be "good for her." The little girl soon saw that her wishes never come true.

Her predicament, then, was that circumstances completely beyond her control made everything she allowed herself to desire automatically unobtainable. She learned that if she did not express her wishes, the chance they might come true was enhanced. She also observed that even if she kept her wishes secret, she might reveal what she wanted by crying when she was disappointed. As a consequence, in order to keep her father from noticing or deducing what her wishes were by observing her tears, she decided that crying was undesirable. Her father basically and consistently enjoined her not to want anything, not to ask for anything, and not to cry when disappointed. This injunction coming from father's Child (C_F) became the little girl's Parent (P_1). This little girl became a woman, but until she gave up her script she carried her father's injunction, "don't ask for anything," inside her Child as a relentless influence which guided every one of her most significant actions. The Parent in the Child (P_1), with its origin in the Child of the parent (C_F or C_M), is called the "ogre" or "witch mother," as well as Adapted Child.

The injunction, or in fairy-tale language, the "curse," is always a prohibition, or an inhibition of the free behavior of the child. It is always the negation of an activity. The injunction reflects the fears, wishes, anger, and desires of the Child in the parent (C_F or C_M). Injunctions vary in range, intensity, area of restriction, and malignancy. Some injunctions affect a very small range of behavior, such as "don't sing," or "don't laugh loudly," or "don't eat too many sweets." Others are extremely comprehensive in range, such as "don't be happy," "don't think," or "don't do anything."

The intensity of injunctions varies in proportion to the consequences of disobedience. Thus, the injunction "don't be happy" can be given with great intensity, in which case the least expression of happiness can bring severe repercussions; or it can be given with minimal intensity, in which case only minor disapproval is expressed when the injunction is broken. The area of behavior that the injunction restricts depends upon the witch mother's or ogre's specific and delineated focus: the injunction might be "don't think," "don't be happy," "don't enjoy sex," "don't show anger," "don't be healthy," or "don't accept strokes," "don't reject strokes," "don't give strokes."

As to malignancy, some injunctions have destructive long-range effects, while others do not. For instance, the injunction of one alcoholic man was "don't do anything but work." This was not only a long-range injunction, but one so malignant that he eventually found himself unable to avoid a job he disliked very much except by completely destroying himself through drink.

On the other hand, parents are always enjoining their children and many such injunctions are neither destructive nor long-range in effect.

Parental injunctions, like curses, are often introduced into a person's life at the day of birth. For example, parents often predict that a certain child is going to be healthy, unhealthy, smart, stupid, lucky, or unlucky. One alcoholic's mother read his future alcoholism in the stars, a finding which she often repeated to him in his childhood. Myths containing the elements of what the parents would like the child to do in life are often passed down to children. One man, who prides himself on being extremely perceptive of other's feelings, was told that as soon as he emerged from the womb he opened his eyes and looked around. Whenever something bad happened to another, he was reminded that he was born on Friday the thirteenth, and could expect bad luck all his life. Characteristically, the grown person believes that his state is fated rather than produced by the parental prediction. The effect a prediction of this sort may have has been amply explored in the concept of the self-fulfilling prophecy.[31] In general, expected behavior is likely to occur simply because it is expected.

Names often subtly suggest to the child what parents expect of him: John, Jr. is expected to follow in his father's footsteps; Jesse is expected to raise hell; Gigi is expected to be sexy; and Alfred is expected to be well ordered and neat.

It is very important to realize the basic defenselessness of the offspring in the face of the witch mother's or ogre's curse. In household situations where the Child ego state P_F or P_M operates as a pseudo-Parent, it can be compared, in more severe cases, with a concentration camp in which a pair of hundred-and-fifty-pound children beat a forty-pound three-year-old. The severity of some of the injunctions found in hamartic scripts cannot be minimized. This point will be discussed further in the chapter on treatment.

The script, then, is a decision the young person makes between his own autonomous needs and expectations, and the pressures or injunctions he encounters in his primary family group. These pressures can be diagrammed in a script matrix (Figure 3B). It will be noted that the influences operating on the youngster are limited by the diagram to influences emanating from the parents. As this diagram implies, culture has no effect on an individual's decisions about his life course other than as it is transmitted specifically by one of the parents or parent surrogates. This view stands somewhere between the extreme sociological one that sees a person's behavior as the result of cultural influence only, and the view that regards behavior as strictly the consequence of intrapersonal dynamics.

CHAPTER FIVE

Decisions

So FAR we have been speaking of the predicament of the young child both through the eyes of the psychologist in terms of injunctions, ego states and pressures, and through the eyes of the youngster in terms of witchcraft and curses, witches and ogres, princes and princesses. It is important to realize that, while the psychologist's terms are more respectable to the professional community, the Child's terms carry the full implications and meanings of the circumstances in which the youngster find himself. Because of this, transactional analysts will speak in terms of the Child as well as in the terms of the adult psychologist. This preference is rooted in the belief that for therapeutic interventions to be meaningful to the patient, they must be meaningful to his Child as well as to his Adult.

Adoption of a script occurs when the youngster's expectations and tendencies are not met. Instead, sources alien to the Child seem to apply considerable pressure in overwhelming ways which, unless yielded to, make life extremely difficult. Thus, the Child is forced to abdicate his birthright and he does this by readjusting his expectations and wishes to fit the situation. This process is a crucial point in the development of scripts and it is called the decision.

The decision is made when the youngster, applying all of the adaptive resources of his ego, modifies his expectations and tries to align them with the realities of the home situation. Accordingly, the decision has two important aspects: time and form.

The process by which the ego realigns itself with the realities of the ego's context has been described thoroughly by Erikson.[14] He calls it the process of ego identity formation. Erikson, in his epigenetic view of personality, postulates that in order to arrive at a proper ego identity, the individual has to master several previous "psycho-social crises." Mastery of each depends on mastery of the previous ones.

In order to attain a healthy ego identity, or life plan, the person has to have mastered a crisis of trust, shame, guilt, autonomy, and productivity. Having mastered these, the individual, Erikson feels, will probably be able to handle the formation of ego identity in an appropriate manner. Erikson implies that failure in one of these previous crises leads to a malformation of ego identity. A script is basically such a malformation.

TIME OF THE DECISION

The decision is a product of the synthetic function of the ego; the age at which it is made varies from person to person. In a life course which develops normally, a decision of such importance as what one's identity is to be and what goals one will pursue should be made late enough in life so that a certain measure of knowledge informs the choice. In a situation where a youngster is under no unreasonable pressure, the identity crisis—or the period of life during which the identity is decided upon—will occur somewhere in adolescence.

A script results from a decision which is both premature and forced, because it is made under pressure and therefore long before a decision can be properly made. In Erikson's view, this means that the process of identity formation is forced to occur not only earlier than healthy development demands, but also is based on improperly mastered previous stages of development. Such decisions are indications of a stressful home situation. It would appear, for instance, that the pathology encountered in autistic children may be based on a very early decision to reject human stimulation because of its stressfulness. In autistic children the stress may not be entirely due to the parents' behavior but also to a defect in the child's perceptual and sensory mechanisms which do not provide an adequate barrier against excessive stimulation.[17] Nevertheless, such an early decision leads to a clearly malignant script.

Psychopathologies can be graded on a list by degree of malignancy, the more malignant tend to be based on earlier decisions in life.

The decision is as good and as viable as the skills of the Professor at the time of the decision. The Professor operates at a different level of logic, perception, and cognition than the Adult of the grownup. In addition, the Professor is forced to operate with incomplete data because of his limited sources of information. In general, the younger the person making the decision, the more likely that the Professor operated on incomplete data and imperfect logic.

Making the decision eases pressure and increases satisfaction. For example, one young homosexual recalls that when he was a little boy his mother showed great discomfort when he played with the rough children in the neighborhood. He also noticed that if he imitated those rough boys, his mother expressed considerable disapproval. He found no support for any boyish behavior from his father who acquiesced to his mother's phobia of manliness and hyperactivity. He wanted to be "one of the boys," but this wish encountered so much resistance and pressure that he recalled deciding on a specific day of a specific week of a specific year that he would be his "mother's good little boy," a decision which very obviously made life easier for him. When he presented himself for treatment at age thirty-five, he was indeed mother's good little boy—neatly dressed, clean, polite, well-groomed, considerate, and respectful. Unfortunately, the decisions which had been adaptive and comfortable at age ten, were, when he applied for treatment, completely anachronistic and responsible for considerable discomfort. The decision had affected his sex life, in that he practiced a sort of depersonalized sex as a homosexual, which was an adaptation to his mother's injunctions. His decision also affected his work because he saw all work as an acquiescence to a motherly demand. This view resulted in a basically childlike approach to his endeavors, always tainted by acquiescence, mixed with bitterness. The bitterness came from the fact that even though he had decided to be mother's good little boy, the decision had been made with considerable anger and resentment.

It might be noted here that traumatic neuroses—a neurosis caused by a traumatic event—fit into this scheme as situations in which the pressures on the youngster making the decision are acute and sudden rather than chronic. Here the crux of the psychopathology is still the decision, but one made in response to an acutely uncomfortable situation as opposed to one made as a result of long-standing and enduring pressures.

Good scripts, or life plans which have socially redeeming qualities (such as the script of a martyr or hero), are premature and forced decisions as well; their outcome may seem to be generally positive, but the decision is made before the appropriate resolution of the necessary psycho-social crises and therefore without the necessary information and autonomy. The corollary of this statement is that decisions which lead to healthy personality development must be both timely and autonomous. Thus, in proper script-free ego formation, the date of decision is such that it provides for sufficient information, lack of pressure, and autonomy.

FORM OF THE DECISION

In Erickson's terminology, the basic position of the infant can be said to be one of *basic trust*. As he describes it, this comes from a situation in which the infant feels that he is at one with the world and that everything is at one with him. It is clearest when mother and child are most basically interacting, as when feeding or nursing at the breast; even more basic is the mutuality of mother and offspring *in utero*.

Transactional analysis would describe this basic trust as the first of four possible existential positions a person can assume. The four positions are "I'm O.K., you're O.K.," "I'm not O.K., you're O.K.," "I'm O.K., you're not O.K.," and "I'm not O.K., you're not O.K."

The original position, "I'm O.K., you're O.K.," is rooted in the biological mutuality of mother and child which provides for the unconditional response of the mother to the child's needs. How a mother responds unconditionally to the demands of a child can be clearly understood by observing a cat and her kittens in the act of feeding. The cat, basically a stimulus-bound organism, is so constructed that when a kitten meows in discomfort the mother will strive to end this discomfort. Thus, the mother cat will seek out the kitten and try to start the nursing process. This can be interpreted as an expression of a mothering instinct, but it can also be seen as a fairly stimulus-bound behavior pattern: the unpleasant meowing of the kitten produces an urge in the mother cat to offer herself for nursing in order to bring about the cessation of the unpleasant stimulus. This example simply emphasizes that there is a biologically given responsiveness in the mammalian mother to a hungry offspring, and that this biological responsiveness almost guarantees a primary mutuality which, in human beings, generates a basic trust or a position of "I'm O.K., you're O.K."

This basic trust position, "I'm O.K., you're O.K.," categorizes what we call the position of the "prince," and this position is one that the infant tends to adhere to.* The only reason a youngster gives up this position for either "I'm not O.K.," or "You're not O.K.," or both, is that the original, primary mutuality is interrupted, and that the protection which at first was given unconditionally is withdrawn. The insecurity of uncertain protection with conditions brings the youngster to the conclusion that either he is not O.K., mother is not O.K., or both are not O.K. Needless to say, this decision is not reached without a struggle. It requires considerable pressure to convince the prince that he is not, after all, a prince and to cause him to believe that he is, instead, a frog. It is important to note the difference between a youngster who feels that he is O.K., but is rather uncomfortable because of the circumstances in which he finds himself, and the youngster who adapts to the discomfort of his surroundings by deciding that he is not O.K., and therefore becomes comfortable. In a situation of this nature, the choice seems to be whether to remain an uncomfortable prince or to become a comfortable frog.

Becoming a frog requires not only a transition from "I'm O.K." to "I'm not O.K.," but also the adoption of a conscious fantasy about the kind of frog the youngster finds he is.

FROGS AND PRINCES, DUCKLINGS AND PRINCESSES

In most scripts the individual behaves as if he were someone other than himself. This is much more than

---

*In transactional analysis, children are seen as princes and princesses until their parents turn them into frogs.

mere dissimulation or surface masking. The youngster who finds himself unable to make sense of the pressures under which he lives needs to synthesize his decision in terms of a consciously understood model. This model is usually based on a person in fiction, mythology, comic books, movies, television, or possibly real life. This mythical person embodies a solution to the dilemma in which the youngster finds himself. For example, one patient, Mr. Salvador, consciously thought he was Jesus Christ, and recalls that as a young boy his parents had accused him of killing his younger brother. Their exact reasons for doing this are not clear, and whether they meant it as a joke or seriously was never understood. However, the patient as a youngster found himself having to make sense of this accusation. Reared as a Catholic he had read the Bible, and he decided that he would redeem himself of his original sin by living a pure life, such as that lived by Jesus Christ. Thus, Mr. Salvador's script was based on the life of Jesus Christ, a good example of the way youngsters synthesize and make comprehensive their home situation by way of a commonly available myth or fairy tale. This identity was consciously maintained by the patient throughout his life, and Mr. Salvador reported that three or four times during any one day he would have conscious thoughts about his Christlike identity. As an example, when he was once seeking an overnight sleeping place at a friend's house and was turned down, he thought, "No room at the inn." On another occasion, at a particularly unhappy time in his life, he severely hurt his forehead which drew blood above his eyes, and he formed a vision of the crown of thorns; once again this was a *conscious* identification. Incidents like this, in which the script's mythical character becomes a consciously understood reference point, are commonplace phenomena in scripts.

While the choice of a mythical character, or frog, that a person can emulate to adapt to his predicament is limitless, it is possible to divide them into three broad types: the Sulk, the Jerk, and the Prick. The Sulk and the Jerk have been described by Berne previously.[5] Briefly, the Sulk has been angry at one or both of his parents since childhood, usually because he was jilted by them. His favorite way of gaining strokes is to sulk in a corner until someone seeks him out and attempts to rescue him. The Jerk is a person whose parents were very demanding and who thoroughly trained him to do the "right thing," namely, what they wanted him to do. His primary way of gaining strokes is always to try to do everything right, and he often winds up as a Rescuer to the Sulk. The Prick is angry at his parents, not because they jilted him, but because they mistreated him. His principal method of obtaining strokes is to attack people and invite them to persecute him. While Sulks are usually women and Pricks are usually men, there is such a thing as a male Sulk and a female Prick. For example, an alcoholic Sulk used to go to a bar and very conspicuously drink alone; his mythical hero was Quasimodo, the hunchback of Notre Dame. An example of a female Prick is a woman who makes a hobby of collecting men and whose mythical heroine is Wonder Woman.

A Jerk is no more likely to be male than female. A good example of a Jerk is a man who chose Othello as his mythical hero and who continually terminates love affairs and friendships because he is unable to accept people's weaknesses. The same slavish adherence to parental wishes for perfection operated in a female Jerk who chose as her mythical heroine the Virgin Mary.

The extent to which persons imitate large areas of the behavior of real or imagined characters varies within three dimensions; reality, complexity, and adaptiveness.

REALITY

Within the variable which may be called reality, the character chosen for imitation can be a highly stylized, completely mythical individual at one extreme, or a live, flesh-and-blood person at the other. Thus, Mr. Junior's mythical character was his father, who had died when he was seven years old. Mr. Junior knew his father partially through his own dim recollections and partially through the bittersweet memories of his mother. At the other extreme of reality, Mr. Nietzsche chose as his mythical character Captain Marvel, as understood by him at age twelve, through his reading of comic books. Mr. Junior, when behaving as he thought his dead father behaved, had a human, flesh-and-blood appearance; Mr. Nietzsche, on the other hand, had an extremely unreal, rigid, and almost robot-like appearance.

COMPLEXITY

The mythical character chosen can vary in complexity. For example, recall Mr. Salvador, who chose Jesus Christ as his mythical character. His view of Jesus was a fairly complex elaboration of what he knew about Jesus at the time he made his decision. He gained his understanding of the personality of Jesus Christ by reading the catechism and the Bible, but his extensive elaboration made his portrayal considerably different from what anyone might expect. For example, as a boy he had come to the conclusion that Jesus "was making it with Mary Magdalen" and that, in general, He was not chaste, but a sexually active man who got involved with females in distress and tended to protect and care for them. His particular understanding of the mythical character was later turned into action and he was therefore quite active sexually with females who required him to protect them. Complexity of the mythical character appears to be a function of the age at which the decision is made and the abilities and knowledge of the youngster making it.

The uncomplicated or lower end of the complexity continuum can be exemplified by Mr. Bruto who based his choice of a mythical character on a painting, *The Man with a Hoe,* which represented simply an overwhelmingly burdened, almost subhuman male. Mr. Bruto consequently lived a life of hard work as a common laborer.

It should be noted at this point that youngsters choosing a mythical character always elaborate the available material and adapt it to fit their own circumstances, needs, and information. Because of this, it is important in diagnosing a script to know how to retrieve the patient's interpretation of the character he has adopted, and not to make the mistake of assuming that the popular version is the one the patient has adopted.

ADAPTIVENESS

The third variable of the mythical character is adaptiveness. While the choice of mythical character is always adaptive to the home situation, that is, to the demands of the witch mother or ogre, it is not always adaptive to the social environment into which the person will grow. Thus, Mr. Cagney, who chose Al Capone as his mythical character, found that the behavior dictated by this choice was adaptive within the small confines of his home. Here, Mr. Cagney's mother, husbandless and angry at the world, expected her son to be tough, embittered, and cold-blooded toward others. However, this behavior became extremely maladaptive as soon as he left his home, not only because the community into which he grew no longer had a viable slot for a big-time syndicate boss, but also because it caused him to value and to commit actions which were distinctly frowned upon by the police. On the other hand, as a young girl Miss Felix chose Marilyn Monroe as her mythical character; she found that this choice was not only adaptive within the home, but also being a sexy, feminine woman whose only wish is to submit to powerful men, was adaptive in the world at large. Another example of a more flexible adaptive mythical character is a doctor, lawyer, or scientist. This choice would probably be adaptive to the home situation as well as to the world at large.

NOT THAT SHAGGY

In relating parental injunctions to the decisions children ultimately make, it is common to find what has come to be known in transactional analysis as the "Not *that* Shaggy" phenomenon. "Not *that* Shaggy" refers to the fact that parents want their children to behave in a certain way, but when the children follow the injunctions, modified by their own elaborations, the parents often are horrified at the results and cry, "Not *that* shaggy!" or in other words, "Oh, my God, that's not what I had in mind!" The phrase comes from a shaggy-dog story in which a prospective dog buyer rejects all dogs brought to him as not shaggy enough. When the buyer is finally brought a peanut-sized dog whose fur fills the living room and trails out the door and into the street as well, he cries in horror, "Not *that* shaggy!" A classical example is the case of Buddy, an eighteen-year-old boy, who decided that "I ain't taking nothing from nobody." This decision translated itself into such extreme sensitivity and violent reaction to pressure from parental figures that he would fly into uncontrollable rages when pushed beyond his limits. These rages were so extreme that he had been hospitalized or confined from age fourteen on. Buddy recalls that as a six-year-old, while chasing his older sister with a butcher knife, his mother reprimanded him by saying indignantly, and in an injured tone, "Buddy, you are *too young* to be chasing your sister with a meat cleaver!" It is clear in this situation that mother, who would consider this kind of behavior appropriate at age eighteen, yelled "Not *that* shaggy!" when Buddy, a precocious young man, engaged in it at age six. Similarly, a man who is sexually attracted to his daughter may urge her to be sexy and hurry up and have intercourse. When he finds himself with a thirteen-year-old pregnant child on his hands, he has difficulty recognizing that the girl had simply followed his instructions, with only minor variations. The same situation is found over and over again in the case histories of alcoholics and other drug abusers who describe their parents' dismay when they discover their offsprings' drug abuse after years of encouraging the use of alcohol or other drugs to deal with stress, and of condoning drug abuse in themselves and others.

CHAPTER SIX

Diagnosis

IN SCRIPT analysis, diagnosis has a purely treatment-oriented purpose. Scripts are diagnosed not in order to attach a label to the patient, but to suggest a treatment strategy.

A basic therapeutic operation in script analysis is Permission. How a therapist gives Permission is explored in the chapter on treatment; at this point it is sufficient to say that Permission is a therapeutic transaction which enables the patient to revoke his decision to follow the parental injunctions. The therapist is aided in giving Permission by a clear understanding of the patient's parental injunctions, their source, and content. He should be able to distinguish the counterscript from a genuine change in the patient's script. Further, he should have a clear understanding of the aspects of the patient's decision affecting his everyday life, namely, his mythical hero, somatic component, and sweatshirt,* as well as his central game. A complete list of relevant

*See p. 62 for the description of "sweatshirt."

diagnostic data will be supplied later in the Script Checklist.

THE INJUNCTION

The injunction tends to come from one of the parents, and observation of a large number of cases has yielded a useful rule for diagnosing its source: the parent of the opposite sex is the source of the injunction. This view is primarily based on clinical evidence but has a theoretical coherence as well. The argument is rooted in the same evidence that led Freud to his conclusions about the Oedipus complex. The mutual sexual cathexis between fathers and their daughters, mothers and their sons, would generate the prediction that, as we have observed, mother "calls the shots" for boys and father "calls the shots" for girls.*

Given the first rule, the next rule is that the parent of the same sex teaches the youngster to comply with the injunction of the parent of the opposite sex. Thus, if mother dislikes assertive behavior in men and boys, she will enjoin her sons not to be assertive and, having married a non-assertive man, will provide her son with a father who gives him the proper example.

Let us illustrate the above with an example of how a young girl might become a beautiful woman. (Figure 4). Mr. America likes beautiful women, that is to say, his Child likes beautiful little girls. He marries a beautiful woman, Mrs. America, and they have a daughter. The little Miss America's Child is told by her father's Child to be a beautiful little girl and is taught by mother's Adult how to do it. Mrs. America knows how to use make-up, how to dress, how to stand, how to talk, since she is herself a beautiful woman, and transmits this knowledge to her daughter. This genesis of beauty, it will be noted, is basically independent

*This rule has been questioned by other transactional analysts, though not convincingly enough for me to abandon it.

of physical attributes. It explains why some women with all the physical attributes of beauty are not beautiful, and vice versa. It should also be noted that many physical attributes such as weight, posture, skin texture, facial characteristics, etc., may be affected by parental injunctions such as "enjoy (food but not sex)," "don't outdo me," or "don't be happy."

Miss America's example illustrates how people marry each other to form what can be described as a child-rearing team. In the same manner as was illustrated above, a woman who has a phobia of assertive behavior will marry an unassertive male and they as a team will produce unassertive male offspring.

Thus, when attempting to diagnose someone's injunction, the working hypothesis for a man is "mother tells you what to do and father shows you how"; and for a woman, "father tells you what to do and mother shows you how." This rule has a remarkable parallel in the folklore that accompanies the raising of fighting bulls. In this highly profitable and competitive business, one of the most important rules of breeding is "the bull derives his fighting spirit from his mother and his strength from his father"—a clear case of "mother tells you what to do and father shows you how." The manner in which the parent of the same sex demonstrates how the injunction should be obeyed is called the *program*.

This rule is a working hypothesis, that is to say, the most likely to be correct given no prior knowledge about the case. Exceptions have been found, but not in more than about one-third of all the cases that have been examined by me.

An interesting characteristic regarding injunctions is how parents who appear to be perfectly reasonable and pleasant people (to the casual observer) are perceived by their offspring as witches or ogres. The reason is that to the outside observer the Child ego state of these individuals has no particular potency,

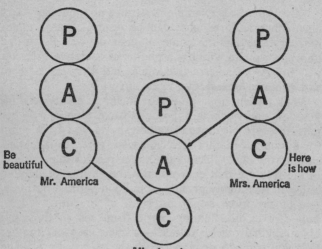

How to raise a beautiful woman

Figure 4

and is therefore regarded in realistic perspective. But to the young offspring who live under the sway of that Child ego state and are unconditionally subject to it, its power and malignancy can be almost supernatural. Thus one sees grown, mature men under the complete control of their old and feeble mothers, or women in full bloom under the total domination of their aging fathers. In treatment this suggests that as long as a person sees his parents as witches or ogres, treatment is not complete, since the person is still reacting to them as he did when he was a child.

After diagnosing the "crazy Child" in mother or father, the next diagnostic task is to decipher the exact outlines of the injunction. It is here that the diagnostician needs to know a great deal about children, childhood development, and child-rearing practices. The diagnostician's task is to imagine himself as an invisible observer in the home situation of the patient. Keeping in mind that the injunctions are often not spoken but implied, hinted at, or thrown out as jokes or when the parents are angry, it becomes possible to reconstruct the specific Child ego state enjoining the patient. With my own patients, I am able to conjure up a vivid image of the home scene as viewed through the eyes of the witch mother or ogre, along with the content of the injunction. Naturally, these mental images are essentially educated guesses and have to be checked out against the patient's recollections, as the patient is always the final judge of the validity of a diagnosis.

THE COUNTERSCRIPT

So far the discussion has focused on the influence of the parental Child ego state on the offspring. Scripts are predicated on a state of affairs in which there is a basic antagonism between the Parent and Child in mother or father. It is because of this antagonism of mother's or father's Parent (P_M or P_F) for their own

Child (C_M or C_F) ego state that their Child (C_M or C_F) seeks expression through the offspring. Because of this antagonism, the offspring is not only given the injunction by the witch mother or ogre, but in addition is always given a contradictory message coming from the Parent ego state of both parents. Thus, while one young homosexual's witch mother enjoined him not to be a man, the Parent ego state of both parents demanded that he be a man (Figure 5A); while an alcoholic's mother demands of him that he drink and that he not think, the Parent ego state of both parents expects him to be an abstainer (Figure 5B). When these two demands are made of a young person, he will basically follow the injunctions of the witch mother or ogre, but the life course usually involves an alternation between compliance to the witch mother or ogre's injunction incorporated in the script, and compliance to the parental Parents or counterscript.

The counterscript is an acquiescence to the cultural and social demands that are transmitted through the Parent. In the alcoholic, the counterscript reoccurs in the periods of sobriety between binges. If one looks back on the case history of an advanced alcoholic, one always finds periods during which it seemed that the script's tragic ending would be avoided. The alcoholic, as well as the people around him, seemed to believe that the tragic outcome that everyone feared had indeed been avoided. This situation, in which the hero of the tragedy seems for a time to escape his tragic end, is an essential requirement of a good tragic script, both in real life and on the stage. Anyone who has seen an ancient Greek tragedy or any modern version of a tragic play knows that regardless of previous knowledge about the outcome, the audience truly hopes and seems to believe that the known, inevitable ending will be dramatically averted.

In contrasting the two sets of instructions given by parents to their offspring, one representing the script

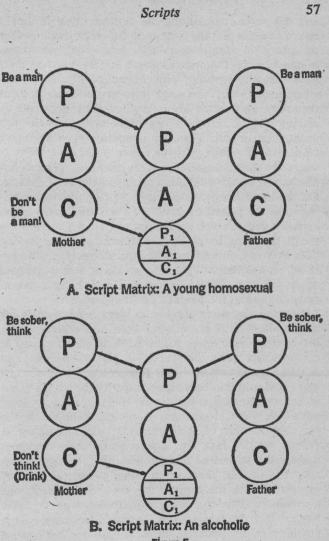

A. Script Matrix: A young homosexual

B. Script Matrix: An alcoholic

Figure 5

and the other representing the counterscript, it should be noted again that the injunction from the witch mother or ogre is in almost every case nonverbal, not transmitted in explicit words. Because of this, most patients have difficulty agreeing with the notion that they were given such injunctions until it is made clear to them that they were often given implicitly by approval or disapproval of certain forms of behavior, or through insinuation or jest. Thus, an injunction such as "don't be assertive," while perhaps never uttered verbally, is made by the consistent reinforcement of passive behavior and negative reinforcement of assertive behavior. On the other hand, the counterscript instructions coming from the parent's Parent ego state are usually given verbally and are not always associated with reinforcements designed to produce acquiescence. The saying "Do as I say, not as I do" characterizes the situation in which the Parent ego state makes a verbal demand of an offspring which is contradicted by the action emanating from the parent's Child ego state.

Because the witch mother or ogre injunction is far more potent and meaningful than the counterscript, the counterscript never succeeds. It is characteristic of counterscript behavior that it is highly unstable and brittle, for the reason that it runs counter to the much more powerful tendency represented by the script. When in the counterscript phase, the person feels a deep, primitive, visceral discomfort, which alcoholics often place in the pit of their stomach; the discomfort is related to the fact that counterscript behavior goes against the wishes of the witch mother or ogre. Consistent with this, there is an equally visceral *comfort* associated with the script behavior. For example, one alcoholic reported that at the worst point of an alcoholic binge, when he was so sick he could no longer keep anything in his stomach, he heard his mother's voice saying, "Isn't this fun, Jerry?"

As suggested in this example, an alcoholic who behaves as the script demands carries out those tendencies in his personality which acquiesce to parental wishes and are therefore associated with the well-being and comfort of parental protection. This is one reason the hangover is seen as the payoff for the alcoholic: even though in pain, the individual with the hangover is receiving approval for acquiescing to the parental Child's injunction. During this period the alcoholic feels temporary respite from the demands of his witch mother or ogre. Although the patient's Parent ego state may be actively castigating him for his drunkenness during the hangover, this does not prevent the observer from realizing that while castigation is taking place, father's or mother's Child is saying, in effect, "That's my boy!" Other aspects of the payoff in the hangover are discussed in the chapter on alcoholic games.

One aspect of counterscripts which distinguishes them from a genuine departure from the script is their unreal quality. For example, it is common to find among black delinquent youths that their script alternates between aggressive delinquent behavior (enjoined by the witch mother) and wholly unrealistic attempts to "make it" in the entertainment or sports world which represents the culturally accepted alternative for "good Negros" (enjoined by the Parent ego states around them). Succeeding in these endeavors is statistically unlikely, and they almost always represent a counterscript. A true departure from the script, or a new life course, cannot constitute being a "good Negro," but usually necessitates well-coordinated, often strongly self-assertive and angry, but realistic approaches to the realities of racism. Such an approach is emerging in the black community in the form of militant youth groups like the Black Panthers. These movements are of great value in that they clearly offer an alternative to the usual self-defeating scripts which are so commonly seen among black people.* The basic message given a black youth by such a movement is "You're O.K., not in spite of being black but because of it. You are a prince and you deserve princely treatment. Black is beautiful. Your hair is beautiful, you are beautiful. You can have anything you want. You are a prince, you are O.K." This statement offered at the time of decision is a powerful antithesis against the adoption of a self-destructive script such as heroin addiction or alcoholism, and is likely to tip the balance for many black adolescents, by giving them permission to be O.K. and offering them a realistic path to the attainment of autonomy.

From the diagnostic point of view during treatment, the principal significance of the counterscript is that the behavior of a person still following his script but in a counterscript phase may be indistinguishable from another person who has in fact given up his script. The alcoholic who has stopped drinking, is working, and seems happy and content may have given up his script or he may be in the counterscript. A therapist who mistakes counterscript for cure is in danger of being a Patsy, as will be explained in the chapter on treatment. On the other hand, a therapist who is unwilling to recognize a cure and insists that it is only a temporary remission is in danger of becoming a Persecutor.

Thus the proper diagnosis is essential here. Diagnosis should always be based on behavior changes. The most convincing change for an alcoholic is a protracted period of moderate social drinking. However, since many cured alcoholics lose interest in alcohol, this criterion is not always available. In general, the loss of preoccupation with alcohol—either the alcoholic pastimes, or the game in any of its roles—it is a good criterion. A radical change in time structuring and the

---

*This point of view was confirmed for me informally by a group of probation officers from Alameda County who have observed a decrease of delinquent behavior in black youths who join the Black Panther Party.

development of avenues of enjoyment without alcohol are crucial indicators of a script change. In addition, an often subtle change in the physical appearance of the cured alcoholic is a reliable index though difficult to assess. The alcoholic in a counterscript is tense, anxious, "uptight," even when smiling and enjoying himself, as if constantly on the brink of relaxing and letting go, which he feels he can't do for fear that his "Not O.K." Child will take over. The cured alcoholic lacks this "on the brink" quality and therefore looks and "feels" quite different from the alcoholic in a counterscript. The tension of the counterscript is a part of the somatic component, to be elaborated upon later in this chapter.

THE DECISION

The decision has a number of components: the existential position or racket that is embraced at the time of decision; the sweatshirt; the mythical hero chosen to live out this position; the somatic component which bodily reflects the decision; and the actual time of the decision.

Knowing the exact date of the decision is useful because it pinpoints the child's age and gives an estimate of the Professor's level of development and understanding at the time the decision was made.

The existential position adopted at the time of the decision represents a shift away from the original basic trust position "I'm O.K., you're O.K." In addition, it is based on some elaboration of either "I'm not O.K." or You're not O.K.," or a combination of both. This elaboration is called the racket because the person will exploit every situation to justify whatever position he chooses. For instance, a woman with an "I'm not O.K." position elaborated it into a "Nothing I do ever works" racket and would use any situation to feel badly. Whenever she went to a meeting she played her racket as follows: If she got there early, she felt badly because she could have used the time to do an additional wash at home; if she arrived late, she would feel badly because everybody noticed her with disapproval; and if she came on time, she felt badly because no one noticed her. Thus, no matter what the situation, she used it to promote her racket.

The patient's "sweatshirt" is intimately related to his decision. The sweatshirt is a metaphoric reference to the fact that most persons with scripts can be visualized as wearing sweatshirts over or under their clothes, on which is written a short, two- or three-word description characterizing their existential positions. In addition, just as games contain a sudden switch or reversal, so sweatshirts often have a front and back. For instance, Miss Felix's sweatshirt, which she wore very tight, prominently read "Looking for a man" in front. On the inside of the back, for anyone who peeled it off, was written "But not you." Captain Marvel's sweatshirt said "Captain Marvel" on the front and "Unless I'm sober" on the back; another man, a born loser, had "You can't win them all" in front, and "I can't win any" on the back.

The mythical hero has been amply described earlier. The diagnosis of the mythical hero, when there is one, is aided by such questions as "What is your favorite fairy tale?" "Who is your favorite person?" "Are you imitating someone's way of life?" and so on. If a certain person or personality emerges as significant to the patient, he should be asked to describe the person fully, since it is the patient's view of the mythical hero, and not the popular one, that is relevant. If the description fits the patient's life—and when it does it often does uncannily—then it can be safely assumed that the mythical hero has been diagnosed. From then on, treatment can be simplified by using the mythical hero's name to refer to script behavior. For instance, every time a patient whose mythical hero was Little Orphan Annie obligingly accepted the "hard knocks of life," a pattern which was part of her script, some group member would call it to her attention by saying something like "That's the way Orphan Annie would take it, but what are *you* going to do?" Or if a man whose mythical hero was Superman muscled his way into a conversation, he could quickly be made aware of his behavior by simply saying "There goes Superman again." Incidentally, identification of sweatshirts, rackets, stamps, and mythical heroes may provide much therapeutic Fun* in the course of group treatment, another reason for the use of these colloquialisms in therapy.

Not everybody with a script has a clearly defined mythical hero. Some persons see themselves as nondescript losers, "Mr. Nobody" or "Nowhere man," and in these cases it is not possible to diagnose a mythical hero. Generally a person with a clear-cut mythical hero is easier to treat because his script behavior is so apparent to the therapist, the group members, and himself.

Another important element in the diagnosis of scripts is the *somatic component.* The somatic component refers to the fact that a person who has made a decision invariably brings certain aspects of his anatomy into play, especially his musculature. Because the script is the result of a negative injunction, namely, the inhibition of some form of behavior, it usually becomes visible as the contraction of one or more sets of muscles. Eric Berne has pointed out the relevance of sphincters,[6] but any muscle, set of muscles, or organ can be involved. This concept, similar to Reich's character armor, finds expression in certain postures (chest out, stomach in, tight anal sphincter, shoulders up, tight lips, crossed legs) which are effective in obeying the parental injunctions and which always have some physical similarity with the fantasied appearance of the mythical hero. Other organs, such as tear glands in the case of Little

*See Fun, p. 172.

Orphan Annie who could not produce tears even when crying, or an accelerated heart rate, can also be part of the somatic component. In this connection it is interesting to note that a decision may be accompanied by changes in any number of vital body functions, which over the years could have definite effects on the person's health.

Many interactions between mental life and bodily functions have been investigated because they can become the cause for physical illnesses. The mechanisms postulated to explain the development of these conditions are mediated by the autonomic nervous system, which responds to states of mind. An early childhood decision may be seen as such a state of mind which then produces certain somatic side effects. A more concrete instance of the effect of a decision can be seen in the following case.* Miss Rein, who had several episodes of urinary tract infection, admitted that she deliberately refrained from drinking water during the day and retained her urine as long as possible because she had decided the bathroom where she worked was dirty. Her own bathroom at home was extensively decorated and was her pride and joy. This woman's attitude about bathrooms and bathroom functions clearly contributed to the development of her recurring bladder infections by allowing the stagnation of urine in the bladder, thus affording the bacteria more time to multiply. Her constant control of the need to urinate was reflected in her posture and could be detected visually, affecting her life hour by hour, day by day, and year by year.

One woman always sat with her legs tightly crossed and arms folded across her abdomen. This self-protective posture was a clue to her decision not to let anyone touch her. Miss Felix, on the other hand, whose script required many superficial sexual relationships, always

*Thanks are due to Dr. George David who reviewed this section and provided the example of Miss Rein.

sat with her back arched and bosom thrust forward, frequently squirming in her chair with a slow, undulating motion. Other behavior, like overeating, smoking, and consuming other drugs, have well-documented effects on the body and can often be tied to a decision.

Thus, observation of the person's anatomy often yields important information about the somatic component of the script and is therefore important in diagnosis.

DOES EVERYONE HAVE A SCRIPT?

A person's life may fit into one of several different possibilities. He may be script-free or he may have a script. If he has a script it may be hamartic (dramatic) or it may be banal (melodramatic). Whether hamartic or banal, a script may be good or it may be bad.

Miss America provides an example of a life course in which no script may be present. Not everyone has a script, since not everyone is following a forced, premature, early-childhood decision. Miss America decides at some point that she is a beautiful woman, but this decision is made at an appropriate age and involves no sacrifice of an O.K. position, loss of autonomy, or inhibition of expectations.

A person with a script is invariably disadvantaged in terms of his own autonomy or life potentials. The distinction between good and bad scripts is based on whether or not it has socially redeeming features. For instance, a man whose script was to become famous but unhappy to the point of suicide, became the most successful surgeon of his city at the expense of a satisfying family life and happiness. This man had a script personally damaging, but socially useful, and therefore it could be called a "good script." On the other hand, a person with a hamartic script such as alcoholism, which is not only destructive to happiness but has no socially redeeming features, has one that is usually known as a bad script. It should be emphasized, however, that in either case—whether a good or a bad script—the fact that a person has a script is a detriment to the possibilities of living life to its fullest human potential.

Scripts can also be divided along lines of dramatic impact. As stated, scripts can be highly dramatic and tragic (hamartic) or they can be melodramatic (banal). In the banal form of script, while autonomy is restricted, it is not so restricted as to be dramatically obvious, and its adoption is far more frequent than the more dramatic, hamartic script. Banal scripts are those often adopted by large groups of people who are treated as sub-groups—such as women or blacks; these scripts are usually based on parental injunctions which are not as severe and restricting as those involved in hamartic scripts. An example of banal scripts is one often found among women, such as "Woman behind the Man"; in this script, a woman decides that she cannot be a full human being unless in some way she has the supporting role in a man's life, so that she never excels in the presence of men, and has no permission to compete or be equal to them.[43] Another banal femal script is "Plastic Woman"; such a script is adopted by a woman who was told that her value depended upon how attractive an object she was, who was enjoined against being intelligent or loving, and who was given permission only to be an attractive object to gaze upon—a duckling in princess's clothing. A woman with this kind of script will constantly endeavor to remain equal to a standard of beauty which she never achieves. She eventually becomes completely encased in plastic, a human being whose only interest is to make a good appearance. The banal scripts that are often imposed upon blacks have been very aptly described by White[42] and, again, they are restrictions of autonomy imposed upon human beings which have melodramatic, rather than dramatic, life outcomes.

Another script—sometimes banal, sometimes hamartic—worth mentioning is one frequently found among "mental health" workers, called "Rescue." This depressive script consists of an endless ride on a Rescuer-Persecutor-Victim merry-go-round that will be elaborated in Chapter Sixteen.

As to the frequency of their occurrence, banal scripts are the rule, hamartic scripts the minority, and script-free lives the exception.

A SCRIPT CHECKLIST

When diagnosing the various aspects of the script it is useful to keep in mind a list of items that form its make-up, colloquially called a script *checklist* (based on an idea by S. Karpman and M. Groder).

Because of the various meanings given to word script, it is suggested that "script" properly refers to this checklist and that ideally, when talking about a patient's script, the observer is referring to the whole checklist rather than to one or a few of the items. On this basis, "White's injunction is 'don't think!' " is more accurate than "White's script is don't think."

The checklist is presented in the order in which the items are most easily diagnosed.

LIFE COURSE

This is what the patient sees himself as doing, or the outline of his life. It should be possible to state it in a succinct sentence such as "drinking myself to death," "almost always succeeding," "killing myself," "going crazy," or "never having fun." The life course is best stated in the first person singular and in language understandable by an eight-year-old to emphasize that it represents the patient's early formulation of what his life course would be. The life course is usually easy to surmise and is almost always revealed in the patient's presentation of the problem. Life courses can be banal or hamartic.

Four sub-items of the life course are the decision, the position, a mythical hero, and a somatic component. The *decision* is the moment when the existential *position* (O.K., not O.K.) was embraced. The *mythical hero* is the character in life, history, or fiction that the person's life course is intended to emulate. The life course is the reaction to a negative injunction and this reaction usually has a *somatic component* which may involve any effector organ such as the tear glands, neck muscles, heart, sphincters, etc.

COUNTERSCRIPT

During periods of the script when the person seems to be escaping the script's life course, he engages in activities which appear to be departures from the script. These activities form the counterscript and represent acquiescence to a cultural and/or Parental demand, such as "being on the wagon," "drinking socially," etc.

PARENTAL INJUNCTION

This is composed of two parts: the enjoiner, the witch mother or ogre, or more generally mother's or father's crazy Child; and the injunction, or curse.

The injunction is thought always to be an inhibiting statement: "Don't think!" "Don't move!" "Don't be assertive!" or "Don't look!" If the injunction is not preceded by "Don't," or if it is too complicated, it has not been distilled to its most basic meaning. Therefore, the injunction "Consume excessive quantities of alcohol!" is probably not the last word while "Don't think!" may be.

PROGRAM

This is how the youngster has been taught by the parent of the same sex to comply with the injunction coming (usually) from the parent of the opposite sex. Thus, if the injunction is "don't think!" the program may be "drink," "fog out," or "have a tantrum."

GAME

This is the transactional event that produces the pay-off which advances the script. It appears that for each script there is one basic game of which all the other games are variants. Thus, for a "killing myself" life course, the game might be "Alcoholic" with variants such as "Debtor," "Kick Me," "Cops and Robbers," all of which produce the same payoff, namely, stamps that can be traded for a free drunk (see below).

PASTIME

This is the social device whereby patients with similar scripts structure time. With alcoholics the game is "Alcoholic," and its various sub-forms or pastimes may be "D.T.'s" "Cirrhosis," "Disease vs. habit," "Hang-over," etc.

It is while playing the pastime that the *gallows trans-action* is likely to take place.* In the case of the alcoholic, White tells the audience about last week's bender while the audience (perhaps including the therapist) beams with delight. The smile of the Children in the audience parallels and reinforces the smile of the witch mother or ogre who is pleased when White obeys the injunction and, in effect, tightens the noose around White's neck.

PAYOFF

Stamps, racket, sweatshirt: The *stamps* represent the kind of effect accompanying the end of the game—anger, depression, sadness, etc. The act of pursuing and collecting the stamps is the *racket*. Every person has his own individualized racket and type of stamps. The *sweatshirt* refers to the fact that people prominently display their racket on their chests, so to speak, as an advertisement to willing players.

*For full description, see p. 166.

TRAGIC ENDING

This is important to therapists treating patients with hamartic or self-destructive scripts. The tragic ending is usually specific as to time, place, and method, and is a sort of *modus operandi* which characterizes each self-destructive individual. Suicidal persons will stick to a certain form of suicide, thus affording the therapist a *script antithesis,* a transactional stimulus intended to disarm the self-destructive injunction. If the tragic ending is death through drinking, the script antithesis includes the injunction "Stop drinking!" plus Antabuse and, in extreme cases, removal of available alcohol by whatever means necessary. The script antithesis does not dispose of the script, but it buys time during which treatment can lead to script abandonment. The script antithesis has been clinically tested in my work with very clear results. The most impressive result of a script antithesis is found when the patient—as he is about to leap off the bridge—hears the voice of the therapist saying "Don't jump!"

THERAPIST'S ROLE

This is the role which the patient expects the therapist to play when he applies for treatment. Alcoholics commonly expect therapists to play the role of Patsy or Rescuer. This aspect of the script will be discussed fully in the section on Treatment.

CHAPTER SEVEN

Theoretical Antecedents to Script Theory

THE PHENOMENA composing the script checklist have been observed in detail by a number of previous investigators in the field.

Alfred Adler's "fixed law of movement" postulates that self-consistency dictates behavior throughout life so that "every problem child, every neurotic, every drunkard, or sexual pervert is making the proper movements to achieve the position of superiority."[1] What Adler sees as the position of superiority is seen in script analysis as the adaptation to the world embodied in the decision. The concept of fixed movement corresponds to the fixity and predictability of the life course of a script.

Johnson and Szurek came to the conclusion that antisocial acting out in children and adults has its genesis in some aspects of the make-up of their parents.[26] Though their theoretical inclination was psychoanalytic, they rejected previous psychoanalytic explanations of the acting-out behavior of the so-called "impulsive character," which postulated that the motive for acting out was a need for self-punishment based on a deep-rooted sense of guilt that originated in childhood: the antisocial acts invited the desired punishment. Another explanation, or series of explanations, was based on the concept that antisocial acting out was due to a lack of love for the parents that causes the wish not to acquiesce to parental dictates. This lack of love was said to result from an initial or pre-existing cold and indifferent attitude on the part of the parents.

Johnson and Szurek postulated intsead that the parents unconsciously encourage the immoral, amoral, or antisocial behavior of the child. They concluded:[26]

> The unwitting employment of the child to act out for the parent his own poorly integrated and forbidden impulses was observed by us at all economic and educational levels, with the frequency, regularity, and predictability of a well-defined psychological mechanism determining human behavior.

Johnson and Szurek also point out that some parents will, in the same breath, give their children a parental command and suggest how the command might be evaded or disobeyed. An example was given to me by Miss Smith who recalls how, as a child on her way to the candy store, her mother gave her a lecture about not being rude to the clerk, not stealing candy from the counter, not keeping the change, and not getting candy all over her dress. She remembered that what she basically understood from the admonitions was that mother expected her to do at least one of these, leaving her only the problem of choosing which. It can be postulated from this that the Child of the patient's mother was basically saying to her, "Here are four things that I would do if I were you, and I would consider it a favor if you did at least one of them."

The basic conditions for this kind of parental behavior are: 1) the parent has a Child (C_F or C_M) that wants to do certain things and 2) these are strongly disapproved of by the parent's Parent (P_F or P_M). A strong disapproval of the Child's wishes by the Parent in the mother or father causes his or her Child to encourage the youngster's Child to do the forbidden acts. If Mrs. Smith is able to encourage her daughter to steal candy from the store, then Mrs. Smith's Child will be guilt free or blameless, at the same time escaping the punishment deserved for wanting to steal candy. Mrs. Smith's Parent, however, will harshly punish the little girl for something that Mrs. Smith actually suggested she should do. Parents who are in good touch with their own Child ego state (C_2 in Figure 2) do not need to have their children behave as their own Child is not allowed to and, in any case, will not punish their offspring for doing what they themselves want to do, thereby avoiding the basic elements of the genesis of a script.

Johnson and Szurek report the case of a father-son situation in which a father, who had lost a job which allowed him to drive all around the country, brought into treatment a young boy with a truancy problem:[26]

> It was striking to observe this father asking Stevie to tell of his most recent escapade, and, when the child guiltily hesitated, supplying an intriguing reminder. The account obviously fascinated the father, who easily prompted the child from time to time. Then, suddenly the father angrily cut off the child . . .

Later in the same interview the father said, "Stevie's really a good kid—he would follow me around the top of a wall fifty feet high." "A smile of tacit but unwitting approval," Johnson and Szurek observe, "often belies a parent's complaint of impulsive and daring behavior of a child brought for treatment." Here they have observed the gallows transaction, in which the Child ego state in the parent clearly encourages behavior that later becomes troublesome. Another ironical example of the same situation is given in the case of a young boy who was brought into treatment for stealing: ". . . the mother surreptitiously secured, actually stole, the key from the boy's diary, and discovered a well-ordered bookkeeping system of amounts extracted from guests' purses . . ." Here again the mother sanctions the duplicity of the son through her own behavior.

Johnson and Szurek find case after case in which sexual aberrations, sexual promiscuity, and murder by young patients were clearly traceable to the fantasies, hopes, and fears expressed by their parents.

It is clear from Johnson and Szurek's approach that they have observed the same phenomena being advanced to document script theory. Because of their psychoanalytic background, they related their observations to superego functioning and postulated that parental attitudes cause "superego lacunae" in the child. What they refer to as unconscious fantasies, hopes, and fears of parents, script theory refers to as the parent's Child. According to script theory these are not unconscious fantasies, but simply the wishes or aspirations of the Child's ego state, which are quite conscious to the parent in question *when in the Child ego state*. What Johnson and Szurek refer to as unconscious permission, script analysis refers to as an injunction. Script theory sees the parent not just giving permission for the acting out but actually demanding it in exchange for protection. Johnson and Szurek accurately observe and imply in their writings that children are basically at the mercy of their parents' wishes but fail to note that parents not only permit their children to act out, but actually enjoin them to do so.

Another author who anticipated the concept of scripts is Erik Erikson.[14] Nowhere in the literature are script phenomena as clearly portrayed as in his writings and it is interesting to speculate why, given the overwhelming evidence of clinical observations, Erikson did not construct a theory of personality around the postulation of consciously made life plans and scripts. His concept of identity is similar, in many respects, to the concept of scripts. Yet Erikson did not regard self-destructive or negative life plans as true identities, thereby failing to apply his valuable insights to them. Rather, he chose to label the situation in which a person fails to choose a positive identity as a state of *identity diffusion* or *role diffusion*. Thus, Erikson regards only those identities that are considered positive or socially acceptable as true identities, and considers all other behavior the result of identity disintegration.

As has been stated previously, the process which script analysis calls the decision has been thoroughly explored by Erikson as identity formation. He calls the formation of an identity the positive or favorable outcome of the major psycho-social crisis of adolescence, out of which, if successful, the young person emerges with a sense of ego identity, which "is the accrued confidence that the inner sameness and continuity are matched by the sameness and continuity of one's meaning for others as evidenced in a tangible promise of a 'career.' " If this psycho-social crisis is not satisfactorily mastered, Erikson postulates, the adolescent will emerge with a sense of role diffusion, a sense which, one presumes, is basically the sense that one has no identity, no confidence that the inner sameness and continuity are matched by the sameness and continuity of one's meaning for others, and no tangible promise of a "career."

Yet elsewhere Erikson refers to a young girl whose "inescapable identity choice" became "to be a suicide," and he also discusses the concept of *negative identity* which parallels script notions.

In his monograph *Identity: Youth and Crisis*,[14] he states:

> On the whole, however, our patients' conflicts find expression in a more subtle way than the abrogation of personal identity. They rather choose a *negative identity*, i.e., an identity perversely based on all those identifications and roles which, at critical stages of development, had been presented to the individual as most undesirable or dangerous, and yet also as most real. For example, a

mother whose first-born son died and who, because of complicated guilt feelings, had never been able to attach to her later surviving children the same amount of religious devotion that she bestowed on the memory of her dead child, aroused in one of her sons the conviction that to be sick or dead is a better assurance of being "recognized" than to be heathy and about. A mother who was filled with unconscious ambivalence toward a brother who had disintegrated into alcoholism again and again responded selectively only to those traits in her son which seemed to point to a repetition of her brother's fate, with the result that this "negative" identity sometimes seemed to have more reality for the son than all his natural attempts at being good. He worked hard on becoming a drunkard, and, lacking the necessary ingredients, ended up in a state of stubborn paralysis of choice.

In other cases the negative identity is dictated by the necessity of finding and defending a niche of one's own against the excessive ideals either demanded by morbidly ambitious parents or indeed actualized by superior ones. In both cases the parents' weaknesses and unexpressed wishes are recognized by the child with catastrophic clarity. The daughter of a man of brilliant showmanship ran away from college and was arrested as a prostitute in the Negro quarter of a southern city, while the daughter of an influential southern Negro preacher was found among narcotic addicts in Chicago. In such cases it is of utmost importance to recognize the mockery and vindictive pretense in such role playing, for the white girl had not really prostituted herself, and the colored girl had not really become an addict—yet. Needless to say, however, each of them had put herself into a marginal social area, leaving it to law enforcement officers and to psychiatric agencies to decide what stamp to put on such behavior. A corresponding case is that of a boy presented to a psychiatric clinic as "the village homosexual" of a small town. On investigation, it appeared that the boy had succeeded in assuming this fame without any actual act of homosexuality except one, much earlier in his life, when he had been raped by some older boys.

Such vindictive choices of a negative identity represent, of course, *a desperate attempt at regaining some mastery in a situation in which the available positive identity elements cancel each other out.* [Italics mine.] The history of such a choice reveals a set of conditions in which it is easier to derive a sense of identity out of a *total* identification with that which one is *least* supposed to be than to struggle for a feeling of reality in acceptable roles which are unattainable with the patient's inner means. The statement of a young man that "I would rather be quite insecure than a little secure" and that of a young woman that "at least in the gutter I'm a genius," circumscribe the relief following the total choice of a negative identity. Such relief is, of course, often sought collectively in cliques and gangs of young homosexuals, addicts, and social cynics.

The reader will recognize the striking similarity between Erikson's observations and the material on scripts presented in this book. Yet, Erikson's path of discovery does not, on the whole, follow the lead suggested by his concept of negative identity, probably because, though he terms his theory psycho-social, he tends to move toward the psychic, unconscious, dynamic aspects of human development rather than the social, conscious, and interpersonal.

A truly social or interpersonal approach inclines a student of human nature to see behavior as the result of environmental stimulation, thus neutral. On this basis, whether depression or medicine, suicide or law, a person always has a "career," an identity. On the other hand, by emphasizing the internal driven quality of behavior, the unconscious-dynamic approach assumes that behavior which represents ego-mastery over internal impulses is "good" and therefore worthy of the label "identity" while behavior which represents lack of mastery of internal impulses is "bad" and therefore distintegrated, diffuse, and not properly termed an ego identity. Script theory, again, regards all life "careers" as the result of ego-mastery and adaptation to the environment, and therefore true identities—whether adaptive or self-destructive, whether or not they are considered to be socially redeeming. Erikson also says:[14]

The synthesizing function of the ego constantly works on subsuming in fewer and fewer images and personified

Gestalten the fragments and loose ends of all infantile identifications. In doing so, it not only uses existing historical prototypes; it also employs mechanisms of condensation and pictorial representation which characterize the products of collective imagery.

These statements closely parallel the process in script theory which says the youngster chooses a mythical hero who, in some way, synthesizes and simplifies the pressures of the situation in which he finds himself. Erikson presents the case history of a boy, reckless and shifting at times, somewhat delinquent now, and traces this behavior to the maternal grandfather, who, as described by Erikson, continually sought ever new and challenging engineering tasks in widely separated regions in the western United States. Erikson describes how this man's daughter attempted unsuccessfully to prevent her son from becoming like her father. Even though she attempted to rear the boy as God-fearing and industrious, she continually defeated this intent by decrying the lack of mobility, geographic and social, of her life with her husband as well as idealizing her father's exploits. This case is a graphic demonstration that injunctions may be transmitted across sexes and generations so that the boy in the case history acquired his grandfather's Child's injunctions through his mother. Regarding the manner in which parents enjoin their children, Erikson states:[14]

The more subtle methods by which children are induced to accept historical or actual people as prototypes of good and evil consist of minute displays of emotion such as affection, pride, anger, guilt, anxiety, and sexual tension. They themselves, rather than merely the words used, the meaning intended, or the philosophy implied, transmit to the human child the outlines of what really counts in his world, i.e., the variables of his group's space-time and the perspectives of its life plan.

The above has been an exploration of some of the clinical observations made by others which script theory attempts to integrate. Clearly, if script theory has any validity, it will have been hinted at by other astute observers of human nature. The evidence is that from Sophocles to Erikson scripts have been recognized for profound relevance to human behavior.

Part III

The Alcoholic Game

CHAPTER EIGHT

Drunk and Proud, Lush and Wino

THE LIVES of some people can be seen as an endless repetition of certain games. One common argument against the originality of the concept of games is that it is just a new way of referring to certain very well-known behavior. Freud's concept of the repetition compulsion certainly refers to the same phenomena as the concept of games. When closely examined, however, the concept of games transcends the meaning of repetition compulsion. The repetition compulsion is an explanation which, in effect, suggests a backward-looking individual. The act which is compulsively repeated—usually a childhood situation that has had a great emotional impact—is an attempt to bring about the resolution of an experience of the past. But, like the god Janus, games essentially look both backward and forward.

In their forward-looking aspects, games fit into a life plan. Seen in this context, their essential meaning comes into relief. For example, to the "Rapo" player whose script involves eventual suicide, the game is an essential aspect of the unfolding of the script. The same game of "Rapo" is played by a person throughout the years from decision to tragic ending.

Berne postulates that every game has a childhood antecedent which is the basis of the game as played in adult life. The game of "Rapo," for instance, has as one childhood example the situation in which a little girl standing in a mud puddle invites a little boy to play. The boy enthusiastically plunges in and as soon as he covers himself with mud she daintily steps aside and walks off saying: "John Brown, you are a mess." One patient recalls how, as a thirteen-year-old, she played a soft game of "Rapo" while being walked home or attending school dances. She also remembers how, as a seventeen-year-old, she insinuated to one of the less aggressive boys in her class that she wanted to be asked to the prom. When he did, she triumphantly announced that she had had a date with the captain of the football team for two weeks. Later in life, she allowed boys to become sexually aroused while parking in a car and enjoyed their confusion and vulnerability under such circumstances. At college, she played the better known form of "Rapo," and after a short marriage during which she played "Frigid Woman,"[5] she began to walk into bars unescorted and became more and more depressed with every "nauseating, filthy drunk" who approached her. While the game is the same throughout her life, it becomes increasingly hard until, in the end, thoughts of suicide seem reasonable. In the "Rapo" player described above, the backward-looking, repetition-compulsion aspects of the game are related to the patient's childhood relationship with her father. In its forward-looking aspect, the game is the indispensable action element without which the script would never come to its final tragic outcome.

This person's life can be seen as a chain of games, one after another. Yet, it is not enough to postulate a chain of games in which every stimulus leads to a response and the termination of every game leads to the initiation of the next one. The sequence of games, all leading to tragic suicide, is not simply a chain of random events, but a purposeful life plan. Every game is part of a preconceived chain leading to a preconceived goal. The "Rapo" player in question thought of herself as a tragic heroine in her teens, and realized at an early age that her end would be dramatic and tragic. In all probability the manner in which the suicide will be perpetrated has already been chosen, and all that needs to be done is to collect enough trading stamps to exchange for a suicide. How soon enough stamps are collected depends on how diligently she plays the game after her initial decision.

Like "Rapo," the game "Alcoholic" is part of a preconceived life plan which unfolds further with each renewed playing. The life game of "Alcoholic" was first investigated by Eric Berne in his book, *Games People Play*.[5] In his analysis of the game, Dr. Berne postulates that there is no such thing as alcoholism or "an alcoholic," but that there is a role called the Alcoholic in a certain type of game. It has become clear since the writing of Dr. Berne's book that persons playing the role of the Alcoholic in an Alcoholic game can be divided into three significantly different types. As a consequence, it appears that there are three different games of "Alcoholic," all of which share certain characteristics in common, but each of which has unique characteristics and each of which is preferred by a certain kind of person. The three games are "Drunk and Proud" (D&P), "Lush," and "Wino." These three games will be analyzed according to the scheme followed in *Games People Play*.[5]

The following notation will be used in the analyses:

Title: The colloquial name of the game and its abbreviation, if one is used.

Thesis: The general course the game follows.

Dynamics and Aim: A statement of the covert psychological motivation and goal of the game, or the Child's reason for playing it.

Roles: The roles, or players commonly encountered in the game. The general game of "Alcoholic" has five such roles: the Alcoholic—It, the Persecutor, the Rescuer, the Patsy, and the Connection.

Examples: 1) An example of how the game is played in childhood.

2) An illustration from adult life.

Paradigm: This illustrates as briefly as possible the critical transactions of the game. The Social Paradigm, is the obvious or overt content, and the Psychological Paradigm, the covert content of the transactions.

Moves: The minimum number of transactional stimuli and transactional responses in the game. The actual game may be much more elaborate.

Advantages: 1) Internal Psychological—how the game contributes to internal psychic stability. 2) External Psychological—how the game avoids anxiety-arousing situations. 3) Internal Social—the characteristic phrase used in the game as played with intimates. 4) External Social—the characteristic phrase or derivative game or pastime played in less intimate circles. Both internal and external social games represent the manner in which the game helps to structure time. 5) Biological—the kind of stimulation, physical or otherwise (stroking), that the game offers to the parties involved. 6) Existential—the existential point of view which the game vindicates.

Relatives: The names of complementary, allied, and related games. The importance of these games is that when the alcoholic stops drinking, he will usually switch to one of these related games.

Antithesis: That behavior which will prevent the game from continuing.

THE THREE ALCOHOLIC GAMES

DRUNK AND PROUD

Thesis: In all three alcoholic games, the Alcoholic transacts from an existential position exemplified by the sentence "I'm no good and you're O.K. (ha, ha)." In all three games the Alcoholic puts himself in a position of being obviously disapproved of, allowing those who disapprove to appear virtuous and blameless when the situation, closely examined, shows that they are not only not virtuous and blameless, but foolish and full of blame. Thus, "I'm no good, you're O.K. (ha, ha)" really means "You're not O.K.," but stated in such a way that everyone concerned will be utterly confused.

The specific thesis of "Drunk and Proud" (D&P) is "You're good, I'm bad (try and stop me.)" Anyone who tries to stop the alcoholic from being bad will end up feeling definitely not O.K., feeling either foolish or angry.

D&P is a three-handed game involving the Alcoholic and a player who alternates between Persecutor and Patsy. The fact that there is usually no Rescuer in this game is one of its key characteristics. A D&P player is basically interested in getting persecuting parents so angry that they show their impotence and foolishness. The game is often played by salesmen and executives with their wives, and for them the game is to punish the wife for her dominating and possessive attitudes. Under the influence of alcohol, a D&P player can engage in extracurricular activities with his secretary, can lose large sums of money at the poker table, and can stay out with the boys until all hours of the night, with complete impunity. When his wife reproaches him the morning after, he apologizes, saying "Boy, I feel terrible about this, honey. I'll try to be good from now on." The wife, until now the Persecutor, has two alternatives. Either she accepts the apology, putting herself in the role of Patsy; or she rejects the apology and continues as Persecutor which, since "It" is contrite and rueful, now becomes quite untenable and makes her seem merciless and bitchy. Since "It" doesn't miss any work, at least not more than anyone else in the office, and manages to keep everything going fairly well, he is not interested in a Rescuer and would certainly not allow one to enter the game. Occasionally, the wife plays Patsy when she agrees to go to an office party and then is forced to witness her husband "under the influence" behaving naughtily.

The D&P player seldom drinks at home, since drinking is only an avenue to misbehavior of another kind, which is essentially an angry gesture of repudiation of the Persecutor. Because the D&P player lacks interest in a Rescuer, he very seldom finds his way into a therapist's office on his own initiative. When he does, usually because the wife threatens divorce, he is likely to engage the therapist in the game as Patsy. Any therapist who misses this point and is willing to analyze dreams or discuss childhood experiences with a D&P player will find, as he becomes increasingly confident that therapy is "making progress," that he is exposing himself to an inevitable and monumental disappointment.

The case of the winking patient is an example of this point. Mr. Lavat, a 36-year-old D&P player, came seeking treatment because his girl friend of many years threatened to leave him if he didn't straighten out. The therapist, inexperienced at the time, accepted his request for treatment at face value and proceeded to undertake the usual exploration of the "reasons" for his drinking. Mr. Lavat stopped drinking and, as far as the therapist could tell, continued sober as the weeks passed. One day the therapist met Mr. Lavat in the waiting room and was greeted with a wink. Because treatment seemed to be progressing satisfactorily, the therapist was unwilling to challenge the meaning of the wink and continued to "do therapy." Every week from then on the patient would meet the therapist with a wink. This continued for several months, during which the patient continued to "make progress" and remain sober. Then, quite unexpectedly, Mr. Lavat's girl friend called up, angry, and questioned what the therapist was up to since Mr. Lavat did not seem to be improving but, instead, was drinking more and abusing her. It turned out that at approximately the same time Mr. Lavat started winking, he also began drinking, and had continued to drink between appointments until the present time. Conned in such an obvious way, the therapist felt quite foolish and realized that he had been playing Patsy in a game of Alcoholic. Mr. Lavat never returned for treatment and the therapist learned a valuable lesson: a winking patient is up to no good. This rule has since proven useful in the treatment of other alcoholics, in whom winks and other subtle, apparently humorous gestures, are tip-offs that the patient is using the therapist as Patsy.

Antithesis: An antithesis for the therapist who suspects that he has become a Patsy in the game of D&P is to wait for "It" to protest his blamelessness, innocence, or sobriety, then say, "I think you're right, Mr. White, I believe you are blameless (or innocent, or sober). Perhaps we should discontinue treatment." If White accepts discontinuation, he is clearly playing a game. If he declines and wishes to continue, the therapist can ask what the purpose of treatment might be, thereby getting a treatment contract from Mr. White which will give him leverage in the future. Very often a D&P player who has been dragged into treatment by his wife is willing to settle for a contract aimed at straightening out the marriage. At this point, typically, it is the wife who demurs, saying, "I don't need therapy, he's the drunk," thus revealing that she feels her blameless position is tenuous. However, if "It" means business, his wife will probably agree to treatment and the worthwhile goal of dealing with their marriage problems can be pursued.

Whenever a D&P player goes to a physician because of severe symptoms, his attitude is roughly "O.K., Doc, here we go again, just give me the shot in the old arm, and the pills. My! Have I got a dilly, ha, ha, see you around." This attitude is disconcerting to physicians who think of alcoholism as an illness and fail to understand that, in this case, the hangover is the payoff for the Alcoholic, giving him a chance to be a "bad boy," escape deserved anger, and disconcert grownups. "You wouldn't hit a sick man, would you, Doc?" is a typical alcoholic's statement which exemplifies the physician's dilemma. He is left with three choices: to be a Persecutor, a reluctant Patsy, or a businesslike Connection whose only concern is making a living for himself.

If the wife of a D&P player wants to stop playing the game herself, her only antithesis is to seek family or group treatment, or seriously to propose divorce unless her husband stops drinking. Any other maneuver is likely to be of little or no use and to become just another move in a renewed game.

This game has a number of non-alcoholic relatives, such as "Cops and Robbers," "Let's Pull A Fast One on Joey," "Do Me Something," "Wooden Leg" (what do you expect with a wooden wife), and "Schlemiel."[5] All of these games involve a player actively trying to make fools of others. They all involve a racket in which "It" complains that people are telling him what to do, and he feels justified in the anger which provides an excuse for his next misadventure.

The young man who plays D&P is common in close-knit Irish families and others of old-country descent. Here the young alcoholic is usually rebelling against his mother's overprotective attitude, which means, in essence, "I'm O.K. (good), and you, my son (because you are a man or because you're like your father) are not O.K. (bad)." Offspring in this situation can safely rebel by saying, "I agree, I'm bad, since I'm a drunk, and you are good (ha, ha)." Every time he gets drunk he provokes his mother into presenting him with ample evidence for the validity of the "ha, ha," since she will, typically, lose control and show her angry, persecuting Child which is definitely not O.K.

This game can be considered a son's rebellion against a mother who insists on appearing blameless when, in fact, she is quite angry at her husband and son. The only way her flaw can be exposed is to "bring her out in the open," and the game of D&P is an effective way of doing so.

Women also play D&P, but when they do the dynamics of the game involve father. Female D&P players are often seen among professional women married to meek men. Most women alcoholics, however, learn to play "Lush," the next game to be examined.

ANALYSIS

Title: Drunk and Proud of it (D&P).

Thesis: The general thesis of all three alcoholic games is "I'm no good, you're O.K. (ha, ha)." The specific thesis of D&P is, "I'm bad, you're good (ha, ha)."

Dynamics and Aim: Guilt-free expression of aggression.

Roles: Alcoholic and Persecutor or Patsy.

Examples: 1) Childhood prototype—"Try and Stop Me," messing with food, telling obvious lies, getting parents angry over trivia. 2) Adult prototype—social drinking and subsequent "misbehavior" of the junior executive, salesman, and their drinking circle.

Social Paradigm (Adult to Adult):

Adult: "I misbehaved last night. I'm sorry. I won't do it again."

Adult: "I don't believe you" (Persecutor), or "O.K., I believe you" (Patsy).

Psychological Paradigm (Child to Parent):

Child: "I was bad and you could not stop me, ha, ha."

Parent: "You were bad and I am justified in punishing you" (Persecutor), or "You were bad and I will forgive you" (Patsy).

Moves: 1) "I'm going out—stay home." 2) "I'm getting drunk—you'll be sorry." 3) "I am sorry"—anger (Persecutor) or forgiveness (Patsy).

Advantages: 1) Internal Psychological—expression of anger. 2) External Psychological—avoidance of blame for anger. 3) Internal Social—"Try and stop me." 4) External Social—"Martini," "Morning After," and "Shot and Pills." 5) Biological—positive strokes from drinking companions and Patsy; negative strokes from Persecutor. 6) Existential—"Everybody tries to tell me what to do."

Relatives: "Cops and Robbers," "Do Me Something," "Wooden Leg," "Schlemiel."

LUSH

Thesis: This Alcoholic game is most often played by a middle-aged married suburban wife or, at times, by a downtrodden, hardworking white-collar employee. It is often played by aging male homosexuals. In each case, it is played in response to sexual deprivation, or as a transactional analyst would call it, a lack of "strokes." The thesis of the game is a variation of "I'm crazy (depressed), you can make me feel better (cure me) (ha, ha)." It is usually played with a partner who is unable, or for whom it is difficult, to give strokes. As a consequence, the Alcoholic's continued drinking is to the partner's advantage since, as long as the drinking continues, his own emotional deficiency and his part in the game will not be exposed. As long as "It" drinks, the partner preserves the appearance of blamelessness while, of course, both know that this is not true. Because of the partner's guilt over his deficiency, he is always ready to switch from Persecutor to Rescuer. This particular game is generally played with three hands: the Alcoholic, the Rescuer—usually the marriage partner, and the almost always present professional, who may play either Rescuer or Patsy. The Connection, while not a major role in the game, is always in the background ready to extend credit, make deliveries, or chat briefly while making an early-morning sale of the "hair of the dog."

The Lush player is basically making a plea for strokes. But because these strokes will not be given by a partner under ordinary circumstances, he settles for the costly strokes that are given to him when he is rescued.

Because the Lush player reacts to strokes, it is customary for him to stop drinking temporarily and to make considerable progress when therapy begins. However, because the strokes from the therapist do not replace the needed strokes from the partner, the temporary progress is cut short just as the therapist thinks the patient is well enough to leave treatment. Clearly, since the patient's progress was based on strokes obtained from the therapist, it becomes important for the patient to remain a patient, a situation that he can easily accomplish by going back to drinking.

While the D&P player typically drinks away from home, the Lush player typically drinks at home. It is characteristic that once under the influence of alcohol, the Lush player will often leave the house to seek out a sexual partner wherever he may be available. This constitutes further evidence for the assertion that the Lush player is starved for strokes; as soon as alcohol knocks out the Parent's prohibitions and Adult objections, he will obtain such stroking under whatever circumstances are available.

Antithesis: The only solution for this kind of drinking is therapy involving both partners and a demand by the therapist that the patient stop drinking entirely. The aim of therapy should be to facilitate a mutual stroking relationship between the two partners, often involving intensive examination of their sex life. When, as in the case of D&P, the partner is unwilling to participate in treatment, because he is afraid of being exposed as incapable of loving, the only alternative is a divorce. A married Lush player whose partner is unwilling to cooperate will be unable to obtain the strokes that are needed without causing himself considerable guilt. Thus, the alternative to joint therapy is divorce from the partner so as to be free to obtain the needed strokes without feeling guilty. Obtaining a divorce is only the first step in treatment since, without further treatment, it is likely that "It" will marry another unloving person. Divorce by itself is probably not a therapeutic move, although it is a requirement for being able to do therapy with a Lush player whose spouse is unwilling to cooperate.

Unlike D&P, which tends to be a two-person game, "Lush" tends to involve many persons from many sectors of society. The general public's antithesis to "Lush" should be to refuse to take the various roles of the game as offered. The Persecutor's anger is usually the result of having played the Patsy or Rescuer, and can be avoided by avoiding these roles. The Rescuer role can be avoided by very strictly limiting one's transactions with a drinking alcoholic to referrals to self-help groups or competent psychotherapists. The Patsy role is avoided by viewing with suspicion any verbal statements by the Alcoholic which contradict visible evidence—"Just one drink and I'll quit," "I'll never touch another drop," "Sober as a judge," "Quarter for a cup of coffee." Those who sell alcoholic beverages and do not want to play the game as Connections will obviously hurt their business. Yet, it is theoretically possible to avoid being a Connection by refusing to sell alcohol not just to the obviously intoxicated but to the known alcoholic, whether still sober, shaky, asking for delivery, or buying alcohol in the morning hours.

The youngest Lush player whose case I have recorded

was fifteen-year-old Johnny. The son of a professional athlete who rescued him every time he got into trouble, Johnny had the whole school system up to the principal, and the police department all the way to the chief, playing Persecutors, Rescuers, and Patsys. Neither his father nor his mother would pay attention to him if he did not misbehave, but their interest increased noticeably whenever he began an episode of "Lush." His mother, a firm believer in psychotherapy, had engaged a psychotherapist who was content to discuss symbolism, dreams, and childhood experiences with Johnny and his mother, and to become an assistant Patsy. Both mother and therapist resisted attempts to discipline the boy on the theory that permissiveness and understanding were needed instead of discipline. Johnny's aunt, an alcoholic living with the family, provided him with liquor by leaving assorted bottles and the key to the liquor cabinet in obvious places. Observing this particular situation and the great pleasure that this young Lush player would derive from it, the great zest and charm with which he and his circle played the game with its pathos and its joys, made observers practically feel that the game was worth playing. This is a characteristic of both D&P and "Lush" in their early stages, before they "go to seed."

"Lush," however, is a depressive game, and the racket of the Lush player is "Nobody loves me." The nonalcoholic relatives of "Lush" are "Kick Me," "Look How Hard I've Tried," and "Psychiatry" (introspective type), as well as such "dry" variants as "Overeating," "Overspending," and "Oversexed," all of which are manifestations of a lack of stroking satisfaction.

ANALYSIS

Title: Lush.

Thesis: "I'm crazy (depressed), you can make me feel better (cure me) (ha, ha)."

Dynamics and Aim: Sexual deprivation and procurement of strokes.

Roles: Alcoholic, Rescuer, Persecutor, Patsy, and Connection.

Examples: 1) Childhood prototype—getting attention by hurting self; making messes, etc. 2) Adult prototype —depressed housewife or overworked clerk drinking at home, generally alone.

Social Paradigm (Adult to Adult):

Adult: "I am unable to control my drinking."

Adult: "I will try to help you control yourself" (Rescuer), or "You're a liar" (Persecutor), or "I know what you mean, have another one" (Patsy).

Psychological Paradigm (Child to Parent):

Child: "I am loveless (depressed) and you can't help me."

Parent: "If you don't ask me to love you, I'll try to help you" (Rescuer), or "Get off my back" (Persecutor), or "Perhaps if you have a drink you'll feel better" (Patsy).

Moves: 1) "Love me—you're a mess." 2) "I'm a mess, love me—I can't love a mess but I can try to help you" (Rescuer), or "I won't love a mess" (Persecutor), or "I can't love a mess but you might try a drink" (Patsy).

Advantages: 1) Internal Psychological—procurement of sexual gratification. 2) External psychological—the Alcoholic's avoidance of his real shortcomings. 3) Internal Social—"Try not to pay any attention to me." 4) External Social—"Psychiatry," "Affairs," "Can't Get Satisfaction." 5) Biological—strokes from husband or wife, strokes from Rescuers, strokes from casual lovers under the influence of alcohol. 6) Existential—"Nobody loves me."

Relatives: "Do Me Something," "Kick Me," "Look How Hard I've Tried," "Psychiatry" (introspective type), and "Dry Alcoholic."

WINO

Thesis: "Wino" is always part of a self-destructive life script. The thesis "I'm no good, you're O.K. (ha, ha)" is translated here to "I'm sick (try and avoid that), you're well (ha, ha)." The game of "Wino" is played "for keeps" because it uses body organs and tissue as counters. The players in this game are narrowed down to "It" and Connection.

In the game of "Wino," "It," the Alcoholic, obtains strokes by making himself physically ill. He is willing to sacrifice his bodily integrity to the point of putting his survival on the line, which practically forces others to take care of him. Under such circumstances, others who come to his aid are basically Connections. "It" may wind up in a soup kitchen or jail where he will be fed and sheltered, or in a clinic, where he will be given tranquilizers and nursing care. In either case, the Alcoholic is physically devastated and therefore entitled to some oral gratification—the payoff in this game. The payoff, existentially, is a confirmation of the position "I'm not O.K., you're O.K. (ha, ha)," or more directly "I'm O.K., you're not O.K." To the Alcoholic, the fact that he must be at death's door to get supplies from people implies that those other people, who are in positions of strength and power, are really not O.K. Thus, these other people become Connections, or the source of oral gratification. Even the policeman who arrests and rounds up skid row Winos is really a Connection. That Winos protest loudly when arrested should not prevent the observer from noting that, in reality, the Wino is getting his payoff at this time and is therefore basically pleased; and that the policeman arresting him becomes the Connection to the hospital or to the jail dining hall. This fact is a *caveat* for mental health workers who feel inclined to join a favorite pastime of Winos, "Ain't It Awful," in which the police are accused of heartlessness and callous insensitivity, while the Alcoholics' payoff in the game is ignored.

The duplicity of this game involves police and the courts, and is exemplified by the following early Monday morning scene in drunk court in a large western

city. Wearily eying a score of assorted Winos awaiting
sentence, the judge went through the following dialogue
with Charlie: "Charlie, drunk and disorderly again."
"No, your Honor, I wasn't drunk, I was just . . ." "O.K.,
O.K., Charlie, I know, how about thirty days in the
county jail." Charlie, slamming his fist into his hand
("Shoot!"), spins around and, briskly walking to the
jail door, winks and smiles at the row of waiting prison-
ers. At the social level it appears that Charlie is being
punished for breaking the law. In reality, Charlie has
once again managed to put a roof over his head with
the complicity of the judge. The judge chooses not to
face this complicity, but the content of his statements
reveals that he feels neither truly punishing, nor forgiv-
ing, but is just providing Charlie with a secure situation.

Antithesis: The best antithesis for this game is to
decline debate about mistreatment by the law and discuss realistic approaches to sobriety and giving up the
game. It should be noticed that in contrast to the game
in "full flower," which has five players, Wino has
basically "gone to seed," and is reduced to a simple two-
handed game. It is unlikely that a "Wino" player can be
given psychological treatment as long as he does not
have a place to live, an occupation, and the will to be
sober. Only then is it possible to "treat" the game with
any likelihood of success. Thus, a clinic that treats the
minority of alcoholics playing "Wino" will be most
effective if social casework services precede any treatment. At the same time, the clinic should avoid playing
Connection by avoiding the indiscriminate prescription
of drugs and vitamin shots, all of which are the payoff
to the Wino on a binge.

The conviction on the part of workers that alcoholics
are hopeless, helpless victims of a horrible disease might
seem well-founded to anyone who has seen a game of
"Wino." The very notion that such severe self-destruction could be called a game brings out cries of protest
from well-meaning but insufficiently tough-minded ob-

servers. However, the evidence shows that even the most severe "Wino" player is capable of stopping his self-destruction; the annals of AA are full of examples. Transactional analysts tend to feel that since alcoholism is a game, a person can choose not to play. Because they believe the alcoholic can affect his own life situation, they tend to avoid expressions of pity, empathy, or even compassion, and insist that the alcoholic take responsibility for his behavior. Transactional analysts will especially avoid that indulgent smile of warm understanding often given the alcoholic just off a binge, as he humorously relates his latest escapade. Colloquially termed the gallows transaction, that smile is an unwitting but very powerful reinforcement of the alcoholic's self-destruction, equivalent to helpfully adjusting the noose around a condemned man's neck. An unwillingness to smile at the alcoholic's tragedy has been seen as unfriendly. However, this refusal indicates, once again, that the therapist has not resigned himself to considering the alcoholic hopeless. This leaves him free to smile at whatever is joyful rather than tragic in the alcoholic's life.

The racket of the Wino is "You get nothing till you are at death's door," and a large number of alcoholism clinics confirm this notion. An agency that wishes to belie this statement can do so by devoting a minimum of effort, consistent with medical practice, to sick alcoholics, while expending most of its efforts on programs for sober alcoholics.

ANALYSIS

Title: Wino.

Thesis: "I'm sick (try and avoid that), you're well (ha, ha)."

Dynamics and Aim: Oral deprivation and procurement of oral gratification.

Roles: Alcoholic, Connection.

Examples: 1) Childhood prototype—crying and get-

ting fed, playing sick and getting medicine, food, etc.
2) Adult prototype—skid row wino and his circle.

Social Paradigm (Adult to Adult):

Adult: "I am sick and need help."

Adult: "I agree, take this medication (or food)."

Psychological Paradigm (Child to Parent):

Child: "I am sick, you have to medicate me (or feed me.)"

Parent: "I suppose I must."

Moves: 1) "Help me"—(no response). 2) (Attempt at self-destruction)—"I guess I'll have to help you."

Advantages: 1) Internal Psychological—procurement of oral gratification. 2) External Psychological—the player avoids confrontation with his devastated condition. 3) Internal Social—"I'm dying, and you have to help me." 4) External Social—"Port, Sherry, or Claret," "Cirrhosis of the Liver," "Jail, Clinic, Salvation Army," "Ain't It Awful" (police brutality, rats and roaches, alike luck, etc.). 5) Biological—strokes from nurses, doctors, policemen, and preachers. 6) Existential—"Unless I'm dying, no one does anything for me."

Relatives: "Junkie," "Speed Freak," "Polysurgery."

Compared with other games, "Alcoholic" has several attributes worth noting. It is a life game in that it is capable of providing its players with a full-time, time-structuring activity. It is also specially "crooked" in that its player's duplicity is difficult to detect. The role of Rescuer, for instance, appears truly humane, and it is not always obvious that the Rescuer is as interested in keeping the Alcoholic drunk as is the alcoholic himself. Because of its deviousness, the game's antithesis is difficult to execute and willing players are easy to find anywhere from skid row to the doctor's office.

"Lush" is usually the precursor to "Wino," but not all Lush players end up playing "Wino." "Lush" takes between ten and fifteen years to become "Wino," and whether a person will make the transition from "Lush" to "Wino" depends on whether his script calls for the type of tissue destruction that characterizes "Wino."

The D&P player does not usually make the transition to "Wino" because, while basically interested in aggressively proving that others are no good, he is unwilling to sacrifice his limbs and body. When his bodily integrity becomes endangered, often after an attack of D.T.'s, he usually stops drinking, or controls it so as to remain intact. At times, the D&P player whose drinking becomes a threat to his physical integrity finds, when he decides to stop, that he is physically addicted to alcohol, and that ceasing to drink is not as easy as expected. This difficulty, often surprising to the alcoholic, is usually overcome after several attempts, a fact that supports the contention that alcoholism as a game is quite different from alcoholism as an addiction. For the D&P player, the addictive aspects of alcohol are of little or no interest, since his primary interest is to anger others with his game. To the Lush or Wino player, tissue addiction is usually a requirement, since alcohol is taken for its tissue-destructive scripts—which "Lush" often is and "Wino" always is.

These three games outlined are specifically related to the drug alcohol; similar games are played with other drugs. Persons who use marijuana, stimulants, or hallucinogens and who are not self-destructive play a game of "High and Proud" (HIP). HIP is a minor variant of D&P, the difference lying in the kind of drug used. HIP is not a self-destructive game, but once again is played in order to embarrass grownups. It is worthy of note that the current adolescent rebellion regarding marijuana has accomplished this aim. The cruel and unusual punishment of arresting and prosecuting casual users of marijuana, in the face of increasing evidence that marijuana is neither particularly harmful nor habit-forming, is forcing defenders of "law and order" into an increasingly foolish and untenable position which causes great delight in the HIP player. The HIP player has seized upon an aspect of the grownups around him that is weak and subject to attack or ridicule, and there is a no more heartily felt "ha, ha" than that of the HIP player when authorities become unreasonable in the pursuit of marijuana users. HIP players very often play "Cops and Robbers" as well, where the payoff is being arrested. One young man reported that he felt great joy when, after being arrested for holding one marijuana cigarette, he was given a one-year felony sentence. He realized that his enjoyment came from the fact that the sentence proved the unreasonableness and foolishness of the authorities who were persecuting him.

The nonalcoholic version of "Wino" is "Dope Fiend" and "Speed Freak." Both of these games are part of hamartic or self-destructive scripts. The difference is that "Wino" belongs to a self-destructive script which usually lasts between twenty and forty years, involving chronic and slow self-destruction, while "Dope Fiend" and "Speed Freak" are part of a script which has a much more rapid course. The use of a needle for the administration of drugs seems to be an earmark of self-destructive scripts. Individuals who inject amphetamines intravenously (Speed Freaks) are similar to Dope Fiends and Winos in that they all are playing a game in which the payoff is that they become so ill that they have to be taken care of. Drug users are aware of the significant difference between the "mind" drugs, taken orally or smoked, and the "body" drugs, which are injected. Most HIP players regard body drugs with contempt because they dislike the physical harm they are capable of producing; Dope Fiends and Speed Freaks feel contempt for the mind drugs because they are "weak" and don't produce a "flash."

A great deal of the literature tends to emphasize the differences between alcoholism and other drug abuse, such as heroin addiction. "Alcoholic" and "Dope Fiend" are very similar in their moves and players. Yet the differences between the games exist and the understanding of each kind of drug abuse requires awareness of the specific differences between games. A therapist who is successful with alcoholics can transfer a great deal of knowledge from his treatment of alcoholics to the treatment of heroin or methedrine addicts. Yet, he cannot be effective until he acquaints himself with the realities that characterize whatever new addiction he investigates and attempts to treat. One important factor in this regard is that just as people explore their social context in search of persons who fit into their games, so do persons who have scripts which involve the use of drugs search for the drug which fits their life plan. Alcohol addiction involves gradual, long-term self-destruction of a socially acceptable sort. Heroin use in the United States almost always involves speedy psychosocial degeneration, and methedrine involves a fulminating physical "burn out." Thus, each drug is selected by the addict with its specific properties in mind in a manner congruent with his life script.

The difference between these three Alcoholic games is vital to psychotherapists, law enforcement officials, and anyone who may deal with someone playing "Alcoholic" or its nonalcoholic variants. Reacting to all excessive drinkers in the same way, while reacting to other drug abuse as if it were categorically different, not only overlooks the reality of the situation, but plays into the Alcoholic's game because it is a confirmation that those who are presumably O.K. and attempting to help are, in fact, quite unaware of the entity with which they are dealing, and therefore quite impotent. This, once again, reinforces the basic position of the game which is, "I'm not O.K., you're O.K. (ha, ha)."

Part IV

Social Significance
of
Games and Script Theory

CHAPTER NINE

The Game of HIP

GAMES AND scripts have a profound personal significance to persons who engage in them. But to regard them as strictly personal and to ignore their larger social ramifications would be to ignore another extremely important aspect of them. The following two chapters address themselves to the broader meaning of games and scripts.

The game called "High and Proud" (HIP) is closely related to the alcoholic game "Drunk and Proud" (D&P). D&P is a game often based on a relationship between a man who is a drunk and proud of it and a woman who wishes to give the appearance that she is without flaw, and who basically conveys the attitude "I'm O.K., you're not O.K." The relationship is one of a bad boy to his mother, Child to Parent, bottom dog to top dog.

The purpose of the game—the payoff for the alcoholic—is to turn the tables on the righteous parent, to get even, to get on top. One alcoholic patient tells about his wife who is a compulsive cleaner, who empties the ashtray without saying a word as soon as he finishes a cigarette, who demands that he take off his shoes when he enters the house to protect the rug. Her general attitude about him is one of Parental contempt for his lack of will power, his weakness, and his many mistakes. This man tells how he would get drunk and rip down the curtains as he held himself up to throw up on the living-room rug; his wife would then lose all self-control and become a shrieking madwoman. While telling this story he would say, with a devilish smile, "The shadow strikes again." By this particular device he managed to put her in the position of demonstrating beyond a shadow of a doubt that, contrary to her claims, she too was not O.K. The next morning he would ask, "Gee whiz honey, what happened last night?" And she'd say, "You threw up on the rug." To which he would answer, "I'm sorry. I'll never do it again." He would then obtain further proof that she was not O.K. because either she would still be furious—in which case she was a persecuting, heartless witch—or she would believe him, which made her into a dummy. The position of the D&P player is "You're O.K., I'm not O.K. (ha, ha)." The player overtly agrees that his wife is, as she claims, O.K. and that he is not. But he always has a smile on his face, and he always says, "I'll show you it's not really that way; you're the one who's not O.K." That is why with "Alcoholic," as with other games, it is often important to watch the smiles of the player because they frequently reveal where the payoff is.

This game is based on a credibility gap, on a discrepancy between how the wife pretends to be and how she really is; the payoff occurs when the alcoholic can show that this woman who pretends to be perfect is in reality not perfect at all. The gap between reality and what the Parent proposes as real is the *sine qua non* of the game.

The game of HIP contains similar elements and has, as a childhood paradigm, a popular fairy tale, "The Emperor's Clothes." In it, the Emperor, after announcing that he's going to wear his latest, most beautiful suit of clothes, parades in the street completely naked. Everyone, including the news reporters, lauds his clothes, but the fact is that he is naked. One little boy alone says, "The Emperor has no clothes." The ending of the story is not clear, but it is obvious that one of two things happens: either the Emperor's guards beat the little kid's head in and that's the end of that, or the people say, "Wow! He doesn't have any clothes on!" and they run the Emperor out of town or make him wear some real clothes.

The game of HIP has come to the attention of the general public largely because of the news media's interest in the "hippie" culture. Being hip is a state of mind and form of behavior that originated in the black ghetto and was, and still is, one of the devices whereby the oppressed black minorities assert their superiority over the white man. It delights an oppressed black person to see a white man with his airs of superiority suddenly come into the realization that he has been made a fool of. The game was taken up, together with the black language which is part and parcel of it, by a large number of young people who were, in time, called "hippies" by the media. The height of this popular youth movement was reached in the summer of 1968 and it is by now almost completely extinct. Young people are now finding other ways to express their needs and ambitions, and most of those who still exhibit the surface characteristics of the hippie era are now either true derelicts on the one hand or "plastic hippies" on the other. Every other hippie-looking person is by now a policeman, and the cultural revolution has moved on to other forms of expression.

The game of HIP, however, remains an interesting phenomenon and because it had its most notorious manifestations in the hippie era it will be analyzed here as played by the hippies of the late '60s. Early in the hippie movement one popular right-wing commentator described hippies as "foul-mouthed, obscene, unpatriotic, hairy drug freaks." This description does in fact hit the highlights of what the game is all about; "Everything they say we are, we are," was the proud response of many a hippie to this description. The game was in fact played with the aid of foul words, marijuana, psychedelics, nudity, and the Vietnam war. Each one of the above items is used in the game, and each one of them contains the essential ingredient for the game which is a vast credibility gap between what grownups say and what is in fact the case.

Let us take hair, for instance. Everyone knows that it doesn't matter how long hair is—George Washington, Albert Einstein, Jesus Christ, all had long hair; but by the simple device of letting one's hair grow shoulder-length and then walking down the street, it used to be possible for a young male to cause grownups to completely lose their composure and to demonstrate, as one young friend of mine put it, that "they are all senile." This device is an elegant variant of throwing up on the rug while tearing down the curtains. The purpose is to create a very strong Parental overreaction, the more absurd the better.

Foul words are used in the same manner. Grownups use foul words in their everyday conversations, and the Constitution guarantees freedom of speech. Yet when a youngster uses foul words like "fuck," especially if it is used in a context which grownups have for some reason defined as being inappropriate, he is going to produce again and again that desired overreaction from them. Thus, by using, under the protection of the Bill of Rights, a common, everyday word relating to an essential bodily function, the HIP player can create a "mind-blowing" reaction in his pompous and hypocritical elders.

Marijuana works the same way. The more research that went into the subject of marijuana the more it became obvious that there was a tremendous gap between what is real and what the authorities were claiming to be real. And as that gap became greater the extraordinarily harsh punishments that were meted out to marijuana users became increasingly absurd.

Nudity and Vietnam were used in combination. When a HIP player disrobed in the midst of a crowd the grownups would say, "You're nude; you're obscene," and the HIP player would answer, "The naked body is beautiful. I'm not obscene. What is obscene is the war. Don't talk to me about obscenity when babies are burned with napalm in Vietnam." Thus, public nudity, refusal to be drafted, and waving a Viet Cong flag in front of a policeman are further maneuvers of this game. All of these situations contain a credibility gap seized upon by the HIP player to turn the tables on the Establishment. In all of them, the Establishment is put in a most irrational and untenable position, much to the player's enjoyment.

The game of HIP can become harmful to the person playing it because in one way or another the person is in danger of sacrificing his body integrity and being beaten, arrested, or fired from his job. But the interesting thing about this game is that when played collectively, it can have socially redeeming features so that it can be called a good game. Seen in this light the game of HIP becomes a good procedure for the "cultural revolution." The cultural revolution needs to be distinguished from the armed, violent revolution. A cultural revolution depends on a three-handed social situation involving a Provocateur, a Persecutor, and a Reasonable Public which basically has the last say in the situation. A good example of a cultural revolutionary move is the Berkeley People's Park situation. The Provocateur found an empty lot and decided to make a park out of it. The overreaction of the Persecutor came just as expected and created a very visible credibility gap. Not only did they not allow the citizens of Berkeley to build a park in which children and pets could play, but they forcibly expelled people from it and built a fence around it. They didn't just say, "You're going to have to move, kids," but by the time one thing led to another the police had shot up about a hundred people, killed one person, blinded another, gassed hundreds of innocent people from the air, and so on. The action by the Provocateur brought out into the open a situation which most people were unaware of, namely that the police were willing and able to go some incredible and illegal extremes in their zeal to defend "law and order." As a consequence the Reasonable Public reacted, and thirty thousand people came to a march in support of the park. The payoff of this game for the Provocateur was to expose the Reasonable Public to the excesses of the Persecutor. As a result of this action, Berkeley now has at least two "People's Parks" and may be the first community in the United States to have a police department which the community controls.

The Kent massacre was similar. As a response to bricks and stones, armed National Guards shot into a crowd of students and killed four. The absurdity of this situation caused such a reaction within the Reasonable Public that the Cambodian invasion that triggered the students' protest was precipitously ended. The Provocateur's action once again brought about an overreaction which exposed a vital flaw in the Persecutors' make-up.

From the point of view of the person who is being beaten or killed by a policeman, the game of HIP is one in which the payoff is related simply to proving that grownups are no good, and it is a situation in which the meaning of the game does not reach beyond its personal significance to the player. From another perspective, when played collectively, it is a very reasonable procedure for the cultural revolution, in which the violence added to the situation by the Provocateur is negligible compared with the violence perpetrated by the Persecutor, and nil in contrast to the violence occurring daily the world over. In either case it is a game requiring courage on the part of the players, because the Persecutor's retaliation is quite unpredictable and physically brutal.

It must be remembered, however, that for this procedure to work there needs to be a Reasonable Public which is made aware of the situation. If there is no Reasonable Public present, then the Persecutor's actions will go unchecked. Let's take a look again at the little boy who says, "The Emperor has no clothes." If there were no Reasonable Public about, he would be beaten up, kicked into the gutter, and that would be that. But with a Reasonable Public witnessing the event, someone will ask, "Why are you beating up that boy?" and that could make a great difference.

Thus the game of HIP provides a procedure for youth and other oppressed peoples to confront their oppressors without a bloody revolution. In a situation where no Reasonable Public exists, an oppressed person can only defend his rights by reacting with force equal to that which is being applied by the oppressor, whereas in a cultural revolution that type of force is not necessary because the Reasonable Public will check the Persecutors' actions.

It is well to note that in the game of HIP what is done is to get the oppressor off balance a bit, and then let him throw himself, as one does in judo. That is the basic difference between a cultural revolution and an armed revolution. The cultural revolution is like judo in which the opponent knocks himself out, while an armed revolution is like boxing where the opponent has to be knocked out by the oppressed.

The above comments on the game of HIP are intended to bring to the attention of the readers some important points. Games are devious procedures which are used by the Child in order to obtain certain forms of satisfaction which are enjoined against by the Parent. In the case of the game of HIP, the satisfaction obtained is the vindication of what the Adult in the Child, the

Professor, knows to be true but is denied by his parents. The game payoff, when played successfully by one person, can be a small consolation for the abuse which may follow in the absence of a Reasonable Public. When played collectively. however, it can become a powerful procedure to systematically reveal the illegality, corruption, and hypocrisy of the elders who run the society.

CHAPTER TEN

After Scripts, What?

OVER THE ages, every new-born cave-age child has smiled expectantly at its "civilized" parents. From generation to generation, humanity has a brand-new chance for self-fulfillment. The new born is enormously adaptable and is capable of surviving the chambers of horrors of its most sadistic fellow men.

Human potential is as infinite as human adaptability. Each generation of parents has the option to oppress its offspring with age-old courses, or to protect their children's spontaneity, encourage their awareness, and respond to their intimate needs that they may reach their full potential. Intimacy, awareness, and spontaneity are innately human and, even if crushed, will re-emerge again and again within each succeeding generation.

Graciously, Mother Nature in this way guarantees ever renewed hope for humanity; without hope for the whole human race there can be no hope for individual members of it.

Part V

Treatment of Alcoholism

CHAPTER ELEVEN

Myths of Alcoholic Treatment

THE PREVIOUS chapters have contained a theoretical exposition of transactional analysis with emphasis on its relationship to alcoholism. Unlike many theories which claim to have explanatory value in the area of alcoholism, this theory generates certain specific therapeutic techniques for treatment. These techniques depart from, and in some places stand in complete opposition to, some of the traditional approaches. There is, in the vast literature concerning alcoholism and its treatment, very little the psychotherapist can use or apply in a practical manner. Most of the literature consists of endless, theoretical statements, shot through with words like compusion, regression, dependency, passivity, masochism, latent homosexuality, underlying psychosis, and so on. All these terms only insult alcoholics and do not seem to answer the question "How do I cure the alcoholic?" Indeed, it is difficult to find in the literature any hopeful statement that alcoholics can be effectively treated, let alone cured. Writings on the treatment of alcoholism are full of general, vague descriptions of treatment techniques, such as "motivating the alco-

119

holic," "family therapy with the alcoholic," "case-work services with the alcoholic," as well as exhortations to use the value of group therapy, psychodrama, and non-directive therapy. Yet at no point does one find suf-ciently specific techniques which have been tried and found effective with alcoholics except, perhaps, for the one hopeful statement by Karl Menninger that the treat-ment of choice for an alcoholic is a thorough psycho-analysis while under confinement.[30] In short, alcoholo-gists are in an ineffectual rut, soothing each other with vaguely encouraging statements with which, as Morris Chafetz has said, "no one can take issue with unless one wishes to be considered against motherhood and for sin."[10]

No treatment approach seems tailored specifically to the alcoholic. If he seeks professional help he will probably be treated through psychoanalytic technique in a one-to-one therapeutic situation, or in some form of group therapy. A notable exception to this state of affairs is the attempt of behavior therapists to develop techniques aimed at removing the symptom of excessive drinking.[19]

As a result of this lack of specific approaches, it is quite difficult for an alcoholic to obtain treatment since competent practitioners, by and large, feel quite un-comfortable and reluctant to treat this prevalent afflic-tion.

This chapter will delineate an approach to the treat-ment of alcoholism that I have used in the last five years with considerable success at both a public clinic and in private practice.

Initially, it will be necessary to review briefly some common attitudes or myths which, in my opinion, tend to interfere with the proper treatment of alcoholism.

THE PARADOXICAL REACTION

It will be shown later in this chapter that a crucial move in the treatment of alcoholism is an insistence on the part of the therapist that the patient stop drinking. This type of therapeutic strategy is viewed with suspicion by most traditional psychotherapists, who would be reluctant to use it for fear of what can be called a "paradoxical reaction." The paradoxical reaction refers to a situation in which a patient who is asked to do something will do the opposite, as a result of being asked. It is argued that it is not advisable to ask a patient to do something such as to stop drinking because it will provoke the alcoholic into drinking even more. It is added that the alcoholic *knows* that he should stop drinking, and that it is unnecessary for the psychotherapist to ask him to do so.

Transactionally speaking, a paradoxical reaction is a very circumscribed phenomenon which may occur when the therapist's Parent either commands or begs the patient's Child to stop drinking. Patients who have entered into a contractual treatment relationship with transactional analysts, when advised of the necessity to stop drinking, have either stopped or not responded; but never in my experience has a patient proceeded to drink more because of this request. This may occur because the transactionally sophisticated therapist avoids the role of Persecutor or Rescuer in the alcoholic game, which is the source of paradoxical reactions; instead, he simply states the necessity that the patient stop drinking.

Some therapists and laymen feel that any attempt to stimulate or provoke in some way the cessation of drinking is a "manipulation" and therefore automatically undesirable. Many laymen will be puzzled by this discussion. Common sense indicates that a psychotherapist will in some way manipulate his patients. However, the myth of the desirability of nondirective, nonmanipulative therapy persists among both laymen and professionals, and needs to be dispelled.

The issue of manipulation will be dealt with briefly. It has long been suspected, and it is now generally accepted, that no therapist can hope to avoid imposing his system of values upon his patient.[23] The issue of manipulation has now become simply a question of whether a therapist, consciously and overtly, is willing to expose his patient to his values or whether he prefers to do it without his own and his patient's awareness. To the transactional analyst, the therapeutic contract makes it clear that the patient wants the therapist to use whatever technique he feels will cure him of his condition, and it is the treatment contract that gives the transactional analyst permission to apply pressures based on his value system. On the other hand, the patient is justified in expecting the therapist to limit the application of his judgments to the confines established by the contract.

One final point regarding manipulation needs to be made. Once the psychotherapist frankly admits that he expects to manipulate his patient, and as techniques of behavior change increase in potency, it becomes extremely important that the psychotherapist obtain a previous, clear-cut agreement or contract,* delineating what the patient wishes to change in his behavior. Practicing therapy without such an agreement or contract leaves the choice of changes to the therapist who will then be clearly overstepping the boundaries of his patient's right for self-determination. No human being has the right, even if he is in the superior position as therapist, to make decisions for another human being, and to do so is more aptly described as brainwashing than as psychotherapy. A therapist must therefore take extreme care to limit his work to areas which are agreed to by the patient.

Closely allied to the issue of manipulation is the issue of "self-discovery." For reasons never clearly specified, it is argued by some psychotherapists that whatever is discovered by the patient on his own is intrinsically

*See Contracts, p. 127.

more valuable than whatever he learns due to the therapist's attempts to teach him. This argument probably stems from observations of the futility of a strictly Parental or exhortative therapeutic approach but it has been extended to encompass any behavior which willfully teaches or transmits information, or which, in one way or another, forces the patient into situations that may lead to self-discovery.

An analogy of approach is that of a man who pushes his stalled car to a gas station and is greeted by a mechanic who, believing in self-discovery, insists that his client deduce the cause and remedy for his car's difficulty. Under the guidance of a good mechanic, the man will probably arrive at a correct diagnosis, and even be able to repair the car, but the joy of self-discovery will hardly compensate him for the expenditure in time and fees that this approach implies.

The critical reader may reply that cars and people are not to be compared with each other and that to think of a therapist as a mechanic working on a car is a travesty of a profound and complex process—yet, I feel that the analogy is basically valid. The services of a transactional analyst are as an expert in human behavior disturbance and its remedy. The cure of alcoholism depends more on the adherence to certain rules to be outlined in this chapter than it does on the marvelous complexities which can be attributed to the therapeutic situation. These complexities, usually subsumed under the heading "the therapeutic relationship," have unquestionable theoretical value but may not be essential for the principal purpose of therapy, namely, a cure. Research in behavior therapy has already found that certain phobias can be cured by replacing the therapist with a tape recorder and a computer.[12] Thus, a therapist can be seen legitimately as a technician who is hired to dismantle people's psychopathology which, incidentally, always represents a mechanization and automatization of behavior. Hence, the analogy of therapist with mechanic is not as far-fetched as it might seem since disturbed individuals do behave like machines and therefore a good therapist might profit from a mechanic's point of view. As the person returns from simple, driven, predictable behavior to the complex, autonomous, and therefore nonpredictable human condition, the therapist—unless he is a guru, philosopher, or busybody—has less and less to add to the situation.

ONE-TO-ONE INDIVIDUAL THERAPY

In the treatment of alcoholism, I think group treatment is a far more potent approach than individual, one-to-one therapy. Because so many variations fall within the category of "group therapy," the minimum standards and desirable features of group treatment will be defined. Group treatment refers to a contractual form of treatment performed in groups of no less than six and no more than twelve patients meeting with a therapist weekly or more often, for a period of time which allows at least fifteen minutes per patient. The composition of the group should be heterogeneous as to sex, age, predominant problem, etc., so that a group will ideally contain no more than fifty percent alcoholics. The group will be seen as the principal and indispensable treatment medium with individual therapy meetings used sparingly but not stingily whenever indicated. Indications for individual sessions are either a crisis or emergency on the one hand, or a situation of heightened productivity on the patient's part such that the time available in group is not sufficient to achieve therapeutic closure. Sometimes individual sessions are desirable, though not always indispensable, at the beginning of therapy because these two conditions frequently prevail. Often patients feel initially that they cannot possibly participate in a group. It is then necessary to "ease" the patient into group treatment through individual sessions, a process which should not take longer than a month.

Individual sessions should not be allowed to become a refuge where the patient can reveal certain matters which he feels are too personal for group discussion. Group treatment implies that treatment occurs *in the group,* and therefore everything that is relevant must eventually be brought to light there. Anything short of that standard will completely emasculate the potency of group treatment, and is usually the result of a belief held either by the patient or by the therapist that the group context is somehow less worthwhile than the one-to-one situation. This belief, whether overtly or covertly held by the therapist, is one of the impediments to successful treatment.

ALCOHOLISM AS A SYMPTOM

Another point of view shared by many practitioners dealing with alcoholics is that drinking is a symptom of a more serious difficulty. This idea, which may have some theoretical validity, fails to take into account some very important and fundamental practical issue. Except, perhaps, in the case of the truly periodic drinker, a therapist who chooses to think of drinking as "only a symptom" and proceeds to ignore it, will have to deal with a patient who, if truly alcoholic, is almost always under the influence of alcohol. It is evident to me that someone who is that heavily drugged is unable to exercise enough Adult control to deal with whatever more fundamental issues are at the root of his drinking. Thus, it is not possible to regard drinking as a symptom and therefore ignore it, and also hope to treat the disturbance. Transactionally speaking, a therapist who chooses to ignore the patient's drinking in favor of dealing with his basic conflicts is playing the role of the Patsy in the game of "Alcoholic," and thus contributing to the perpetuation of the basic conflict.

In addition, it is quite clear that even if drinking is just a symptom, its cessation is a desirable and indispensable first step in treatment. Even though the cessation of drinking does not represent a cure, it does represent a temporary arrest of the progression of the script and as such is a desirable state of affairs in itself. In addition, sobriety seems to be the only context in which a patient will find enough ego autonomy to pave the way for his Adult to come to grips with the fundamental issues that cause his drinking.

ALCOHOLISM AS AN ILLNESS

Finally, the notion that alcoholism is a medically related illness is also an obstacle to its proper treatment. One must not confuse illness, which is one of the many effects of excessive drinking, with excessive drinking, which in itself is not an illness in the medical sense.* Attempts to treat alcoholism with drugs have to date shown very little promise even though drugs prove quite successful in certain stages of treatment.[21] There are presently no drugs specific to alcoholism, nor do drugs show any promise of becoming curative agents in this problem. Instead they are helpful technical aids in the overall psychotherapeutic approach.

*In my work I have received criticism for rejecting the value of the medical disease model, on the one hand, while using medical terminology (therapy, therapist, patient, cure) on the other. This is a valid criticism. For one who wishes to avoid irrelevant medical terminology in psychotherapy, a dilemma exists because there is no crisp, clear-cut, alternative vocabulary. Words such as *counseling, enabler, client, self-actualization* are second-class words chosen for the primary purpose of politely staying out of the way of "real doctors." Until a satisfactory nonmedical vocabulary of psychotherapy is developed, I will continue to use the words that, for the time being, convey a potent therapeutic approach.

CHAPTER TWELVE

The Contract

DRAWING UP a contract is the indispensable first step of transactional analysis group treatment. Transactional analysis is a contractual form of group treatment which needs to be distinguished from any number of activities which may be undertaken in groups and which may be of therapeutic value. When practiced in a group, observing a boxing match or football game, finger painting, dancing, or expressing feeling, can be therapeutic as well as antitherapeutic. The basic difference between therapeutic activities and group activities is the contract. This section defines the therapeutic contract and presents a practical approach to obtaining one.

Therapeutic contracts should be regarded with as much respect as are legal contracts in courts of law, and the legal aspects of contracts are fully applicable to therapeutic contracts.* Legal contracts must contain four basic requirements to be legally valid. Inasmuch as these requirements have been historically evolved

*Thanks are due to Mr. William Cassidy who first suggested to me the similarity that should exist between legal and therapeutic contracts.

from innumerable litigations over hundreds of years, they may be accepted not only as legally necessary but also socially desirable when establishing a therapeutic contract.

MUTUAL CONSENT

Mutual consent implies an offer by the therapist followed by the patient's acceptance. The offer must be explicitly communicated and certain in its terms. The offer made by the therapist is an attempt to ameliorate or cure a certain state of affairs or disturbance. In order to make an intelligent offer, the therapist should know the nature of the patient's problem and it is his duty to elicit this information during the beginning stages of treatment. Thus, the patient should be made to state what he wants to be cured of, in specific, observable, behavioral terms. In the case of the alcoholic, this obviously involves gaining control over drinking and this specific, observable behavioral change is a good basis for a therapeutic contract. On the other hand, the attainment of happiness, better relationships, self-understanding, emotional maturity, responsibility, and other vague achievements, sometimes expressed as the desired effect of treatment, cannot be used in a therapeutic contract because these terms are unclear and nonspecific. In general, it is not possible to enter into a therapeutic contract on the basis of such desired but vague goals and, generally speaking, words of more than two syllables are largely unusable in contracts because of their vagueness. In order for a contract to satisfy the requirement of mutual consent, it is necessary that both parties be able to specify to what they are consenting. Since the patient often has little knowledge of what constitutes the therapist's offer to treat him, he may grasp at any offer no matter how unclear. The therapeutic offer should contain a clear description of proposed services, and the conditions which will be considered to constitute the fulfillment of the contract.

When the patient has no clear understanding of the offer, it may be advisable to arrange a short-term contract of some four to six weeks' duration during which the therapist can explore and diagnose the patient's situation, and the patient can acquaint himself with the therapist and his methods. After the short-term contract elapses, the final offer and acceptance, which implies mutual consent, can be attempted again.

This issue of mutual consent is particularly relevant in the treatment of alcoholics, since it is not uncommon for an alcoholic to misunderstand the therapeutic offer as well as to be unclear in his acceptance of it. For instance, many alcoholics come into treatment due to pressures applied by family or through the courts, and a therapist may make the mistaken assumption that there is mutual consent in the ensuing relationship. The basic transactions of mutual consent are 1) request for treatment, 2) offer of treatment, and 3) acceptance of treatment. It is not unusual for a therapeutic relationship to develop which is lacking in one or more of these transactions. Consider, for instance, the following conversation taking place in the first interview with an alcoholic patient:

Therapist: What brings you here, Mr. Jones?
Mr. Jones: I'm here to get treatment for my alcoholism.
Therapist: Fine. I will be able to see you weekly on Monday at 10:00 A.M.
Mr. Jones: O.K., I'll see you next Monday.

This conversation may seem a satisfactory achievement of mutual consent. If examined closely, however, it may turn out that the patient's "request" was as follows (if one reads between the lines):

Therapist: What brings you here, Mr. Jones?
Mr. Jones: (My wife is threatening to leave me and I

have a drunk-driving charge against me, and my wife and my mother and the judge say I need treatment, so) I am here to get treatment for my alcoholism.

This is not a request for treatment and it probably constitutes a beginning move in a game of D&P. There is only one response the therapist can make which would not further the game, and that is to make explicit the fact that the patient is not requesting treatment. On the other hand, consider the following conversation:

Therapist: What brings you here, Mr. Jones?
Mr. Jones: I'm drinking too much, I have made myself physically sick, I'm losing my wife, and I am in trouble with the law. I want to stop drinking so I am here for treatment.
Therapist: Fine, I will be able to see you weekly on Monday at 10:00 A.M.
Mr. Jones: O.K., I'll see you next Monday.

This constitutes a request for treatment but not an offer, in that the therapist has in no way stated what he intends to do or what he hopes to accomplish. Therefore the patient is free to assume whatever he pleases about what the therapist's role will be, and he will probably assume that it will be one of the game roles.

This could easily be the first move in a game of "Lush," in which the therapist will eventually wind up as a Rescuer. Any further interaction between the patient and the therapist without clarification of the contract would further the game.

The therapeutic offer by the therapist implies that he is willing to treat the problem and that he feels that he is competent to do so with success. Occasionally a patient will request treatment for a condition which the therapist is not competent to treat, at which time it is the therapist's duty to decline making a therapeutic offer. Alcoholic patients on occasion apply for treatment of a minor problem but do not want their alcoholism to be included in the contract. Making an offer to treat a relatively minor disturbance such as marital disharmony without treating the alcoholism can be compared with doing plastic surgery on a terminal patient and should be declined on the grounds that alcoholism is such a destructive form of pathology that it will disrupt and defeat any efforts to deal with minor disturbances.

The above view should not be confused with that held by some therapists, i.e., it is improper to make an offer to treat a symptom such as drinking, sexual impotence or frigidity, or a phobia, because these disturbances are caused by "deep" dynamic disturbances—and treating the symptom will not only be of no value to the patient but, in some mysterious way, may be harmful instead. The argument runs approximately as follows: "This young lady requests treatment to overcome her sexual frigidity. But her incapacity to enjoy sex is related to a deeply buried hostility against men which will overwhelm her if she in fact enjoyed sex. Therefore we cannot offer to treat her frigidity but must treat her hostility instead." This strange sequence of thoughts, not usually communicated to the patient, has a certain similarity to the situation in which a person goes to a store to buy a whiskbroom and emerges with a five-year contract for home maintenance, a vacuum cleaner, and a one-year supply of soap.

Finally, consider the following conversation:

Therapist: What brings you here, Mr. Jones?
Mr. Jones: I'm drinking too much, I have made myself physically sick, I am losing my wife, and I am in trouble with the law. I want to stop drinking so I am here for treatment.
Therapist: O.K., Mr. Jones, I will accept you in treatment. While you are in therapy with me you will be attending group therapy once a week, and perhaps an occasional individual session. I will expect you to stop drinking entirely as soon as possible and will expect you to con-

tinue to abstain for at least one year since it is my experience that individuals who do not abstain for a year tend not to recover from alcoholism. If you remain abstinent for a year while in therapy, you will probably be cured, that is to say, you will gain control over your drinking to the point that drinking will no longer be of concern to you. This treatment implies that you will be actively pursuing not only sobriety but any number of other states of affairs which might be conducive to a cure. I, as a therapist, will be guiding you but the responsibility for your situation has always been and will always be yours. I will be able to see you on Monday at 10:00 A.M.

Mr. Jones: O.K., I'll see you next Monday.

This highly condensed example contains a request for treatment, an offer, and an acceptance, and satisfies the requirements of mutual consent in a therapeutic contract.

VALID CONSIDERATION

Every contract must be based upon a valid consideration. Valid consideration refers to benefits conferred by the therapist and by the patient which may be bargained for and eventually agreed upon. The benefit conferred by the therapist in treatment should always be an attempt to ameliorate or cure a disturbance. The cure of disturbance is defined as follows: Given that a patient and a therapist specify an undesirable state of affairs in observable, behavioral terms, a cure presents a state of affairs in which the patient, the therapist, and the majority of the members in the group agree that the problem described by the patient at the beginning of treatment is no longer present. As a consequence, it becomes clear that it is impossible to state that a patient is cured unless the condition from which he was to be cured was precisely described at the beginning of treatment. In addition, it is quite clear that the "disappearance" of a certain problem needs to span a period of time in which the problem does not manifest itself. For instance, mere sobriety is obviously not a cure for an alcoholic, since most alcoholics go through periods of sobriety at regular intervals.

The only completely valid verification of a cure involves observation of the "cured" patient for the rest of his life. Short of this goal, a cure can be implied from the changes in the person's personality. From a transactional point of view a cured alcoholic not only has had his drinking under control over a period of a year but no longer plays alcoholic games or pastimes, that is to say, does not structure time around alcohol. This implies that he is not playing any of the roles in the game of "Alcoholic" or a variant of it, and that he has effectively overcome the parental injunctions not to think and whatever other injunctions contributed to his alcoholism.

The benefit conferred by the patient is usually monetary. In addition to monetary benefit, a patient must confer an effort toward a cure as part of the consideration. This effort becomes the *only* consideration in the absence of a monetary consideration. Regular attendance and active participation are an indispensable consideration but are often not sufficient since in many cases they are not an effort for the patient. In addition to these, the patient's consideration should involve the performance of tasks, colloquially termed "homework," between appointments.* The performance or nonperformance of this task is often the only measure of valid consideration on the part of the patient, and should always be requested since without it the contract itself is invalid and therapy will probably not come to a satisfactory completion.

COMPETENCY

Contractual ability is limited in certain cases:

1) *Minors.* Legally, minors cannot enter into a valid contract. The likelihood of establishing a contract with

*See "homework," p. 183.

such a person is very slim, unless the parents enter into the contract as well. This necessity arises in treating a minor as it often occurs that the legal guardians will, for one reason or another, decide to discontinue his therapy—particularly if the patient begins to exhibit some changes after a period of treatment. Frequently this decision is based on their notion that the patient is getting worse, instead of better. This phenomenon is easily understandable in terms of the script, since it is assumed that children who need treatment are performing according to the wishes of their parents. When they cease to behave according to parental injunctions the parents will interpret this change as a negative effect of the treatment.

Thus, with minors it is important that at the beginning of treatment a contract be made not only with the minor but with his parents as well. In practice I have found that this difficulty is adequately dealt with by an agreement with the parents that the child will not discontinue treatment unless both he and the guardians consent to it.

2) *Incompetence.* Those whose mental faculties are so impaired that they are incapable of understanding the consequence of their agreement cannot enter into a contract and are therefore not appropriate patients for contractual treatment. Persons who cannot cathect an Adult ego state, such as acutely psychotic individuals or profoundly retarded individuals, are included in this group.

3) *Intoxicated persons.* Intoxicated persons are a subgroup of incompetents and represent persons under the influence of mind-altering drugs to the extent that Adult ego functioning is impaired so as to prevent mutual consent. Contracts entered into while a person is intoxicated are invalid and therefore patients who cannot stop drinking long enough to present themselves to a therapist while sober are not appropriate choices for contractual treatment. It should be pointed out here

that persons who are excluded from entering into a valid contract for reasons of competency are not necessarily unable to profit from other therapeutic measures available to practitioners. The above statements apply only to contractual treatment, which is only one of the avenues available to alcoholics who want to alleviate their condition.

LAWFUL OBJECT

The contract must not be in violation of the law nor against public policy or morals, nor should the consideration be of such nature. This stipulation seldom applies but must be considered with care in the treatment of users of illegal drugs or persons with criminal involvement.

CHAPTER THIRTEEN

Sobriety

GIVEN THAT a patient enters into a contract to cure his alcoholism, the therapist should now concentrate all of his efforts on bringing about a cessation of drinking. Many alcoholics recognize, either through the influence of AA or by their own insights, that they have lost control over their drinking, and that the best approach to their difficulties is to stop drinking entirely. These patients have a distinct advantage over another category of patients who hope that they can arrest their alcoholism without a complete cessation of drinking. These latter cases should be advised of the low probability of their achieving a cure of their alcoholism while drinking "socially." In my experience, no patient who has failed to remain sober for at least a year has achieved a cure. However, it should be stressed that this is not an absolute finding, and that an exceptional patient might indeed be capable of this feat. This must be recognized by the therapist in order to avoid unnecessary disagreement with the patient. Another way of looking at this is to recognize that categorical statements such as "It is impossible to overcome alcoholism without ceasing to

136

drink" will be judged by the alcoholic as persecutory and could easily become the beginning move in a game of "Alcoholic" between the patient and the therapist.

Patients who recognize that it is desirable to stop drinking entirely as a prerequisite to treatment can be offered disulfiram (Antabuse) as an aid, and a good number of patients will accept this recommendation.

Antabuse is a drug which, in combination with even small amounts of alcohol, produces severe and very uncomfortable symptoms. It is taken daily but is effective for as long as ten days or more after the last dose. It is, therefore, a very effective deterrent against impulsive drinking since the alcoholic has to plan days in advance if he wishes to start drinking again.

The use of Antabuse has been much maligned and merits some discussion. Because of unsophisticated prescription of Antabuse in its early days, there exists a prejudice against its use today. Where the alcoholic is forced to take this drug or is even given it without his knowledge, Antabuse therapy is likely to be of no value whatsoever, except perhaps as a deterrent in institutional situations. Antabuse therapy without any psychotherapy may be successful in some cases, but to the extent that the patient's script does not change, it will probably represent only a temporary counterscript in his life. The use of Antabuse as a punishment in conditioning therapy has been unsuccessful because proper conditioning requires that the punishment immediately follow the act which is being punished and the Antabuse reaction takes at least minutes to take effect. Because of its early lack of success and because of the risk of possible death for the alcoholic who drinks "on top" of the heavy doses of Antabuse initially recommended, physicians are reluctant to prescribe it.

The use of Antabuse, however, can be of great value and the risk of death greatly minimized when administered with proper care. At the Center for Special Problems, a public health clinic in San Francisco,

Antabuse therapy has become routine. With very few exceptions, any patient who wants Antabuse is prescribed the drug; those refused usually have a recent history of its misuse, or have a medical condition which makes the threat to the patient's life in case of an Antabuse reaction more severe than the threat of his alcoholism. After being given the appropriate warnings, the drug is dispensed. No attempt is made to produce the Antabuse reaction in the clinic. The initial dosage is 500 mg. (one tablet) per day for seven days which is then cut down to 250 mg. daily. With this approach there have been no known deaths due to Antabuse nor has there been any report of severe or near death reactions in the five years of its use. A certain percentage of patients experiment by drinking a small quantity of alcohol. Most of them are quickly convinced of the drug's effectiveness and stop experimenting. Occasionally a patient reports such a small effect that he was able to continue drinking. In such cases, Antabuse therapy is discontinued.

It has been noted that women are more likely to be willing to take Antabuse than men and the frequent refusal by men seems related to their wish to be strong and to be able to control their drinking without the help of a drug. Typically, a male patient who feels this way will say, "I would like to be able to do it without the help of a crutch," and upon closer examination will admit that this has something to do with his wish, based on conceptions of male adequacy, to be strong and capable of controlling his impulses by himself. The wish for independence from other persons is often the result of a parental injunction against asking for help and, ultimately, for strokes. Patients who recognize the need to stop drinking entirely but do not wish to take the drug should be assessed of the fact that success, while possible, is likely to be jeopardized when sobriety is attempted without Antabuse. Yet, once again, arguments over this issue should be avoided to prevent the persecutory situation described above concerning the complete cessation of drinking. In my experience, a number of alcoholics have successfully stopped drinking without the aid of Antabuse. If the goal of sobriety is achieved, there seems to be no advantage in achieving it by one method over the other.

A patient's willingness to stop drinking depends in part on the therapist's attitudes and transactions on the subject of sobriety, and the treatment strategies suggested in this chapter effectively maximize the patient's actual willingness to stop drinking. Conversely, practitioners who find their alcoholics unwilling to stop drinking may, by virtue of their treatment strategies, be minimizing their patient's actual willingness to stop drinking. Judging from the success shown by most patients, the transactional analysis approach has the effect, from the outset, of increasing the likelihood of sobriety.

Similarly, practitioners who may have found difficulty in introducing Antabuse to their alcoholic patients will feel that the above statements ignore the great resistance of alcoholics to Antabuse therapy. In this connection Dr. Ted Olivier reports that before using transactional analysis he found that less than ten percent of his 140 patients were willing to take Antabuse, while after the adoption of transactional analysis less than ten percent of his 24 patients have refused it.[33] Thus it appears again that the transactional analysis therapeutic approach increases the likelihood of eliciting the willingness to completely cease drinking.

The above statements may seem puzzling or even ludicrous to some readers, particularly those who think of alcoholism as illness. "This approach is based on having a patient who is willing to cease drinking," they will say; "but since the problem of the alcoholic is precisely that he cannot or does not want to stop drinking, this approach is of limited value and an evasion of the facts." This criticism can be answered as follows. Drinking is an act of will: those who want to continue to drink cannot be stopped. However, many alcoholics are motivated to remedy their situation and are willing to stop drinking, and this treatment approach maximizes the likelihood of a cure for those people, when other approaches may actually minimize it. I would never attempt to treat the minority of patients who truly do not want to stop drinking. To the extent that a person is in possession of his faculties, he has the freedom to do as he chooses, and there seems to be no approach at this time which is effective with the alcoholic who refuses to stop drinking.

While the majority of alcoholics are willing to stop drinking, it is not always true that they will do so immediately upon being advised of this necessity. Alcoholic patients who agree to the treatment contract but do not stop drinking entirely will fall into two broad categories. One category of patient will continue to drink steadily and attend meetings under the influence of alcohol; the other will reduce his drinking input and confine it to weekends or to periods between sessions.

The patient who continues to drink steadily and attends a therapy session under the influence of alcohol should be told that individual psychotherapy is useless under these conditions, and that because it represents a waste of time, the therapist will not indulge in it at all. The same is true of attempting to do therapy in group, yet the patient is not only welcome to come to the group if he is under the influence of alcohol, but is required to, even though he will not be allowed to take up any significant amount of time or to disrupt the proceedings. Both of these rules are based on the fact that a person under the influence of alcohol is unable to cathect the properly functioning Adult ego state which, after all, is the fundamental tool of therapeutic improvement. A patient under the influence of alcohol will, on occasion, reveal certain important aspects of his Child, but it is unlikely that any therapeutic work can be done under those circumstances since what occurs will have no effect on future Adult behavior, and most of it will be forgotten. On the other hand, the reaction of the group and the therapist to the intoxicated patient, who is basically in his Child ego state, will be clearly remembered by the patient. Thus, the therapist avoids playing the Persecutor by welcoming the patient into the group, even when intoxicated, and he avoids playing the role of Rescuer or Patsy by refusing to "do therapy" with intoxicated patients, either in individual psychotherapy or in group. Patients should not be seen in an individual session when intoxicated since it is impossible to spend time in that situation without playing the Rescuer or Patsy. Patients presenting themselves for their individual therapy hours under the influence of alcohol should be gently but forcefully appraised of this fact and should be lovingly eased out of the consulting room. Most alcoholics who attend sessions while drinking will, in all honesty, argue that they are able to think more clearly when under the influence of alcohol. The therapist, however, should be quite clear about the fact—supported by a great deal of research, the results of which are available in any standard pharmacology book—that a person under the influence of alcohol is unable to think as rationally as when sober, and he should therefore insist on this point. It should be recognized that the alcoholic's subjective feeling that he is better able to think under the influence of alcohol has an objective basis in the fact that alcohol releases the Child. This sense of release is interpreted as an increased capacity to think, when it is in reality only a disinhibition of the Child ego state.

The second category of patients who drink between meetings presents a somewhat different problem. At first they might attempt to drink and not let the therapist know of it, or even lie about and conceal drinking bouts. This type of patient usually plays the D&P variety of "Alcoholic" game and is basically putting the thera-

pist in the role of the Patsy. By concealing the facts of
his drinking he is attempting to see whether the therapist is interested enough and knowledgeable enough to
actually pursue the matter and confront him with his
actions. If the therapist does not, the patient will probably get his payoff in the feeling that the therapist is
really not O.K. since he is a dummy. When treating a
patient like this, the therapist should make sure that
he remains aware of the quantity and extent of the patient's drinking between meetings. This is accomplished
by questioning the patient and by being receptive to
whatever information may be volunteered by employers,
friends, and relatives. Remaining aware is the best
antitithesis against playing the role of Patsy and it is
because of this that employers, friends, and family are
encouraged to communicate with the therapist. This is
done openly and above board, and with the understanding that information about the patient will not be
divulged without his permission. In this manner, confidence is preserved while awareness is maximized.
Many therapists treat the patient's relatives with a certain aloofness verging on contempt. This attitude is
usually rationalized as being needed for the sake of
preserving the patient's trust but is in reality persecutory and wholly unnecessary. Instead, it is best to
accept information as offered with the proviso that it
must be evaluated and used with caution.

Needless to say, the patient who continues to drink
between meetings without any effort to control his
behavior is basically attempting to place the therapist in
an impossible position out of which he can only emerge
the victim, either as a Rescuer or Patsy. If, however, the
therapist declines this role in the game, and continues
to focus on the drinking issue, he will be playing the
antithesis to the patient's game of "Alcoholic," thereby
making it possible for the patient to opt for an alternative course of action, namely, an earnest attempt
at treating the alcoholism. The eventual result when

a therapist takes this course of action is that a patient will either cease drinking entirely, within three months, or he will frankly and openly admit that he is not interested in changing his drinking behavior and discontinue treatment. In my experience, a very low percentage (approximately 5%) of alcoholic patients who enter into a contract, frankly do not want to cease drinking; they openly say so, and therefore discontinue treatment.

CHAPTER FOURTEEN

Treatment of the Newly Abstaining Patient

ONCE AN alcoholic has stopped drinking, treatment takes a dramatic turn; until then, it is primarily addressed to the problem of helping him to stop.

The first predictable phenomenon after an alcoholic stops drinking is a profound change in the quality of his consciousness, which in many cases is the source of great alarm for the patient, and in most cases makes him, at the very least, uncomfortable. This *withdrawal panic* is particularly pronounced in persons who have had a long history of uninterrupted drinking. Patients who have been on a steady diet of alcohol for many years without ever decreasing consumption and who suddenly stop drinking altogether are likely to report very disconcerting changes of consciousness in the second or third weeks of sobriety.

The withdrawal panic should be distinguished from the *withdrawal sickness*. Both of these crises are the consequence of stopping the consumption of alcohol, but the withdrawal sickness is mostly physiological, a truly medical condition (especially in the extreme case of delirium tremens or D.T.'s, which is potentially fatal and usually requires hospitalization), while the withdrawal panic which comes weeks later is not. It should be noted that withdrawal panic may come whether or not there has been a withdrawal sickness. The pattern is usually: 1) withdrawal sickness (if any) lasting not more than a week, followed by 2) a lull lasting about two weeks, sometimes less, during which the Parent ego state is dominant and during which the alcoholic feels very strong and confident, the classic example of a counterscript. This is the well-known period when the alcoholic is "on the wagon" and feeling "on top of the world." This period is followed by 3) withdrawal panic (if any) in which the alcoholic's Adapted Child becomes scared and anxious about the mental changes which occur due to the continued lack of alcohol.

Not all persons who stop drinking undergo a severe withdrawal panic. Patients who do, and who are not on Antabuse, are likely to drink at this time, or if they do not drink, are likely to become obsessed with thoughts of drinking and the struggle against these thoughts. In such cases, the altered state of consciousness is not as obvious to the patient or to the observer as it is with patients taking Antabuse. Persons taking Antabuse are essentially not tortured by the wish to drink. Not preoccupied with this struggle to avoid drinking, they become aware of the change caused by the absence of alcohol in their bodies. One patient reported waking up in the middle of the night with uncontrolled thoughts racing through his mind which somehow threatened to cause a mental explosion or breakdown similar to a short circuit in a computer. He felt an extreme awareness of minute bits of his wife's behavior, or of having insights into motives, persons' conversations, or of seeing things such as trees and flowers in an alarmingly sharp and vivid way. All of these symptoms, because of their newness and unfamiliarity, caused a great deal of anxiety and he interpreted them in malignant terms. To him, this development meant that he was about to lose his mind or go crazy.

Therapists familiar with this withdrawal panic have at times interpreted it as evidence that, in such cases, alcoholism serves as a defense against the breakthrough of an underlying psychosis. The notion that alcoholism often serves to protect the alcoholic from a pre-existing psychosis is based on the observation that often, after the withdrawal sickness subsides, some alcoholics exhibit clearly psychotic symptoms, such as auditory hallucinations or paranoid states. It has also been noted that certain alcoholics are able to maintain sobriety with the help of drugs of the phenothiazine family which are often used as antipsychotics.[32] These alcoholics are then thought to be basically psychotic and only incidentally alcoholic. This determination may have several outcomes depending on the practitioner making it. The patient may be henceforth ignored as incurable, maintained on drugs but ignored otherwise, or he may even be allowed to go back to drinking since, it is argued, alcoholism is the lesser of two evils. It is therefore quite clear that any diagnosis of an underlying psychosis is not to be made lightly. I always assume that such symptoms are temporary and will subside, usually within one month. In the instance of the patient described earlier, and many others who have gone through similar symptoms, this was the case. I have seen very few cases in which inebriation indeed served as a defense against psychosis. The majority of the patients who go through symptoms of this sort are in the grips of a withdrawal panic and are by no stretch of the imagination psychotic, but simply experiencing an Adult ego state free from alcohol which is so unfamiliar that it is frightening and difficult to assimilate. From the point of view of the script, a patient who stops drinking is going against the parental injunction that he not use his Adult, and that he not think. While a patient is drinking, he is in a

Child ego state, which is acquiescing to the injunctions of his Parent. The withdrawal sickness and consequent feeling of well-being represent a period in which the patient's Parent ego state is regnant and during which the Child willingly withdraws. Withdrawal panic represents a gradual cathexis of the fully functioning Adult ego state; this state of mind which the patient may have never experienced before is a development not only unfamiliar but also frightening, because it is a mode of functioning which was strongly enjoined against and disapproved of by the alcoholic's parents. Therapists should, at this point, provide Protection for the patient by reassuring him that what he is experiencing is an Adult free of the influence of alcohol, and that within a few weeks he will become accustomed to it and will be able to assimilate this new view of his world.* Reassurances of this sort are usually quite effective in helping the patient deal with his panic. At this time it is possible to prescribe a minor tranquilizer to help him deal with his panic temporarily, but this dulls full awareness of the unencumbered Adult ego state and covertly reinforces the parental injunction against Adult thought. Because of this, the use of medication is discouraged unless absolutely necessary.

Additional symptoms that have been observed during the withdrawal panic are dizziness, loss of balance, insomnia, nightmares, extreme cold, extreme hunger, blurred vision, and feelings of being clairvoyant or telepathic among others.

Following this period of panic, if the patient does not evade it by drinking, there is usually a "honeymoon" in which the patient becomes accustomed to his drug-free Adult ego state and during which he feels genuine relief and well-being. The "honeymoon" tends to include a moratorium on the games and the script of the patient, and may last as long as three months. However, it can

*See Protection, p. 177.

be expected to subside, and even though the patient may remain sober, it is always the case that he will eventually resume the games which are allied to his specific game of "Alcoholic" and that his script, whatever it is, will begin to manifest itself in a nondrinking context.

Every patient who has been an alcoholic and has stopped drinking will be faced (as is anyone who gives up a major game) with an existential vacuum relating to the many hours each day which he needs to structure, and which he cannot structure as he did when he was drinking. For instance, many alcoholics who stop drinking attempt to continue structuring time in the familiar way by going to a bar after work. Needless to say, this is questionable since a person in a bar is exposed to all sorts of pressures in the direction of drinking, which he may not feel at first but which will eventually become quite strong. Patients on Antabuse often attempt this approach and because of the drug will not drink, and subsequently may eventually stop this method of structuring time. Other patients who are aware of the difficulties of attempting to structure time in old ways will just find themselves completely at a loss and unable to find satisfactory new methods. A therapist who proposes to help such a patient must aid him in finding ways to structure time and insist that he put them into effect, as part of his homework.

For example, in one case a schedule of concrete activities was constructed to cover every waking hour of the day for a whole week. In another case, a patient who was very shy and reluctant to contact friends was asked and helped to make several calls from the therapist's office to arrange various activities and dates. The underlying purpose of structuring time, as was pointed out in Chapter One, is to obtain strokes which are no longer obtainable through the social contacts involving drinking. Many alcoholics find that when they stop drinking and remove themselves from their alcoholic circle they become solitary and lose the few sources of strokes that they had when they were drinking. The resulting depression due to this loss of strokes is very common at this point in treatment.

In the case of patients who are married and have children, there is usually an increased positive interaction corresponding with the "honeymoon," eventually yielding to a period in which it seems that the members of the family not only expect, but almost seem to wish, that the alcoholic would resume drinking. This phenomenon is easily understood when one remembers that alcoholism is a game and that a game requires several players to be sustained. The wife and children of the alcoholic, full participants in the game of "Alcoholic," feel a vacuum in their lives when the alcoholic stops drinking, equal to that which is felt by the alcoholic himself. Thus, the alcoholic in a family will feel an even stronger urge to drink because, in addition to his own internal proclivity, he will feel the pressures applied upon him by his family. Because treatment of a married alcoholic requires bringing about change in two or more people, it appears at times that the single alcoholic has a better prognosis in treatment. This very real difficulty which is added to the treatment of the alcoholic by the presence of a family is usually overshadowed by the positive influence that families are able to provide. I have sometimes thought that a certain alcoholic might profit by a separation or divorce from his spouse because of the difficulties mentioned above, only to find that if this difficulty is worked through, the family is a great adjunct to the patient's health as a source of strokes and as a basis for existential meaning.

The patient who achieves sobriety by taking Antabuse ordinarily wants to stop taking it within six months. This event should be regarded with suspicion. Most patients feel that after six months of sobriety without the desire to drink it is no longer necessary to take Antabuse. In addition, they yearn for the feeling of autonomy and self-determination that is implied by not having to rely on the drug. However, as soon as Antabuse is discontinued the patient will almost always begin to think about drinking which may start his drinking again. It has been my experience that every alcoholic, after some months of sobriety, drinks again. In the context of ongoing treatment, this episode need not be disastrous, but rather may refresh the patient's memory about the realities of the drinking situation. Except for the patient who goes on an extremely self-destructive binge, one or perhaps two such relapses can have some positive and salutary aspects. The nature and extent of the drinking episode is usually a good indication of whether or not the treatment is having any effect on the patient. By and large, these episodes are shorter and less severe than the previous episodes, and this represents improvement in Adult control. If the patient goes on a binge which is as bad or worse than previous episodes, this indicates that treatment has not been effective and that the patient is only making superficial "progress," with no improvement in Adult control. Patients who are improving will emerge from the episode considerably the wiser for it, in that they will have had a chance to review the different aspects of their drinking in a situation of improved Adult consciousness and control, an experience which invariably proves to be sobering.

In this connection it has been pointed out by Zechnich that discontinuing Antabuse as well as having the first "social" drink after a long period of sobriety is regarded by the patient as a public declaration that he is now "O.K."[44] Because it flies in the face of his household gods, the witch mother or ogre, such an event is always a potential trouble spot. The therapist has to treat such landmarks in the patient's life with finesse, being neither a Patsy who blindly accepts it as a harmless act nor a Persecutor who predicts certain doom. The best attitude is one of the Adult wait-and-see, backed up by a promise of Protection no matter what happens.

Thus, far, this chapter has dealt with some technical procedures found effectively in the beginning stages of treatment. These considerations are relatively independent of transactional analysis theory and are dictated by common sense. They are presented here because certain heretofore uncritically accepted points of view about alcoholism have prevented most practitioners from applying common sense to its treatment. The following section is an exposition of the application of script analysis to alcoholism.

CHAPTER FIFTEEN

Alcoholism and Script Analysis

EXCEPT FOR D&P players, alcoholism as a script or a blueprint for life is usually self-destructive or hamartic. Alcoholism as a clinical entity has as its most striking characteristic the evidence that the alcoholic seems to be willing to actively, consciously, and repeatedly damage himself.

Not all scripts are hamartic, in that not all scripts fulfill these requirements of "good" tragedy. As pointed out in the chapter on alcoholic games, some alcoholics who are not interested in tissue self-destruction are not involved in a hamartic script. A certain percentage of alcoholics and all seriously suicidal persons, however, are hamartic and the same is true of most "needle" drug users, some overeaters and some excessive smokers. Hamartic individuals play hard games involving human tissue. Many alcoholics do not have tissue destruction as their major aim. These nonhamartic, or banal, alcoholics play for depression, anger, guilt, confusion, etc., and the life course of their scripts is not so much "killing myself" as "nothing ever happens," "going from bad to worse," "wasting away my youth," or "losing everything." The importance of distinguishing hamartic from nonhamartic alcoholics lies in the fact that they may require different degrees of therapeutic intervention. The various kinds of therapeutic interventions that are possible for a therapist will be outlined later. At this point, suffice it to say that the treatment of persons with hamartic scripts *requires* "tissue responses" from the therapist.

By tissue response is meant a whole range of responses from the Child and Parent which, in the past, have been purposely avoided by therapists because of their potential danger. These dangers will be elaborated later but briefly, they are behavior in the roles of Rescuer, Persecutor, Patsy or Connection, as well as the gallows transaction. The gallows transaction is a good example of a tissue response which comes from the Child and is harmful, while Fun, which also comes from the Child, is subtly different and essential in the treatment of alcoholics. Thus, while nonhamartic scripts may yield to primary Adult therapy, hamartic scripts require tissue responses.

It has been pointed out previously that scripts are the result of parental injunctions; and injunctions may be classified as to malignancy. Hamartic scripts are the consequence of strongly malignant injunctions and, in the case of a person whose script involves the abuse of mind-altering drugs (including alcohol), a basic feature of the injunction is always "don't think," or in transactional analysis language, "don't use your Adult." Persons who decide on an alcoholic script find that the use of alcohol is a sure method of acquiescing to this parental injunction. For example, one patient reports that as a child he repeatedly witnessed his mother yelling and cursing at his father for his laziness and irresponsibility. At the same time, he frequently saw his mother being lazy and irresponsible, and he recalls perceiving a gross inconsistency in his mother's behavior. One day he asked her, "Mother, how come you're mad at father for not mowing the lawn when you always have a pile of dirty dishes in the sink?" This candid observation made by the Professor—the patient's Adult (A_1) when he was a little boy—was met with mother's strong and angry disapproval. "You get sassy with me one more time, boy, and I'm going to knock your head off." This statement was a clear and forceful injunction against the use of the budding, logical capacity of the youngster's Adult and had the effect of severely inhibiting any more of such thinking in the patient. The same patient found out later in life that it was not as easy to ignore certain painful logical interferences while sober as it was while under the influence of alcohol. Thus, alcohol served to make the parental injunction, "don't think," easier and more comfortable to manage. Thus, he repeatedly chose to drink rather than to think about situations which were very upsetting. For instance, he had considerable difficulties at work which undoubtedly could have been solved had he applied a certain amount of Adult reasoning to them, yet he would suffer through his difficulties at work waiting only for the moment, at five o'clock, when he could rush to the bar and have his first of a long series of nightly drinks. In this patient's case, as in the case of many other alcoholics, alcohol is a means for obeying the injunction "don't think!"

The source of the injunction, "don't think!" is a parental Child ego state which feels "Not O.K." and does not wish to be observed for fear that it will be found out. Thus, "don't think!" is often accompanied by "don't look at me!" "don't talk about me!" "don't talk about us," and eventually, "don't talk about yourself." Alcoholics often find it very difficult to discuss themselves, particularly in groups, and this can usually be traced to these kinds of injunction. As a result, treatment of alcoholics often requires, at the outset, Permission to think, to talk about his parents, and to talk about himself.

A variant of the "don't think" injunction is the concept familiar to skid row alcoholics: the "alkie hex" brought upon those who talk about their accomplishments. The notion is that talking about something has a negative effect upon it. This is similar to the negative connotation of thinking; and not thinking and not talking about crucial situations are always associated with alcoholism.

It might be argued that alcoholics are often rather effective talkers and thinkers. This myth of the quick-thinking, fast-talking, hard-drinking alcoholic does not stand up under close scrutiny. In reality, alcoholics and other drug abusers tend to think and talk in repetitive if wide circles. The facility and quick pace of this kind of talk is related to the release of the Child rather than to any capacity to think about and discuss themselves in a systematic and well-ordered manner.

Hamartic psychopathology or self-destructive behavior is conventionally thought of as an impulse disorder; the "defect" is seen as located in the ego, which is unable to control the impulses at this point. Thus, an alcoholic is traditionally described as a person with an oral impulse to drink which the ego is unable to control. From the point of view of script psychology, however, self-destructive behavior does not imply defective functioning of the ego, but an effective or adaptive mode of ego-functioning. In the case described above, drinking was an adaptation to the parental injunction not to think, and it effectively brought about a situation in which the little boy was able to obtain parental protection. In can be said that a person is "required" to be self-destructive because as a youngster his parent's Child required this in exchange for protection. The person's ego is not defective because it cannot control impulses, but only, if this can be called a defect, because it has more to gain by obtaining protection from the parent than in its own self-preservation. Chapter One postulated that there is a motivating factor called "position hunger" which is a variation of stroking hunger, and represents the need for internal strokes from the Parent. To acquire strokes from his mother, the little boy above was required not to think about certain things. When he made his script decision, his idea that not thinking was a way of insuring parental strokes became part of a consciously pursued behavioral mode, backed even by slogans such as "one picture is worth a thousands words," and "he who hesitates is lost," all of which served to support his decision not to think. From then on, he obtained internal reassurance from his Parent ego state. In this manner, strokes from internalized parents override the normal self-preservative tendencies of the youngster so that the patient avoided thinking in order to preserve his position, a tendency which persisted until he gave up his script by overcoming the internal Parent with the aid of the therapist.

In addition, the alcoholic usually achieves the desired reaction of significant people in his social circle, which most often occurs during the hangover period; the proposition that symptoms are strategies to control the behavior of others is thoroughly explored by Haley.[24] This is why it is said that the alcoholic game's payoff occurs at the time of the hangover. Being so sick that you can't go to work, provoking your husband into a rage, forcing a reluctant physician to administer drugs, or forcing someone to take care of you, are all different forms of the payoff in the alcoholic game. Obtaining these various responses from other persons reinforces the drinking pattern, strengthens the alcoholic's position, and confirms the childhood decision. Thus, the self-destructive ending of the game is sought by the person not as an end in itself, but because it is a requirement for the acquisition of certain strokes or reinforcement, not only from the people in his social environment, but as has been stated previously, from the internal Parent.

As soon as the therapist can see that self-destructive drinking is not the result of a defective ego but a deliberate strategic maneuver to accomplish certain ends, he will be much better able to treat alcoholics.

CHAPTER SIXTEEN

How to Avoid Playing the Game

THE THERAPIST'S job is, first and foremost, not to play the "Alcoholic" game. That is to say, he should not play any of its roles—Persecutor, Rescuer, Patsy, Connection—in order to avoid providing the patient with a payoff from the therapist himself. This is the bare-bones necessity of alcoholism therapy, and the following chapter explains how therapists may play the different roles of the game with their patients.

PERSECUTOR

Enlightened psychotherapists, by virtue of their training, are unlikely to play this role overtly. The tendency among therapists is away from the role of Persecutor, at least in the initial stages of the game, even though a therapist who leads off by playing the game of Rescuer may find himself switching from Rescuer to Persecutor when the going gets rough. The irritation a therapist may feel after repeated failures to help his patient may express itself in subtle ways, such as an exaggerated rigidity in dealing with the payment of fees or the granting of appointments. The role of the Persecutor can also be played in group therapy by subtly discriminating against the alcoholic's statements or by failing to notice or even pay attention to him. A therapist who feels anger toward a patient is in a position of being "hooked" into playing the Persecutor role and because of the strong professional taboo against persecuting the alcoholic, he is probably going to do it in a subtle and therefore insidious manner, which can cause a great deal of trouble.

The therapist who insists on the need to continue treatment when a patient has given up his script is playing the role of the Persecutor as well. This persecutory role is also often played by individuals in AA ("Once an alcoholic always an alcoholic") and other self-help organizations. While a person who feels truly "O.K." will discontinue treatment whether the therapist approves of it or not, the therapist's attitude can nontheless undermine a tenuously held "I am O.K." position by feeding into the witch mother's or ogre's point of view.

RESCUER

The role of Rescuer is more often played by therapists in treating alcoholics. Because a psychotherapist is basically a professional rescuer, it is important to distinguish Rescuers from rescuers. A good analogy can be found in the following situation: A lifeguard is a rescuer hired specifically to rescue people from the sea if they are in danger of drowning. He is trained, physically able, and has at his disposal a number of props—boats, ropes, paddles, life preservers—which aid him in doing a competent professional job as a lifeguard. He sits in his tower, thereby providing a feeling of safety for swimmers until someone is in danger of drowning. He then proceeds to rescue the drowning person and usually succeeds in doing so. If he succeeds in saving the victim's life, he feels good about it; if he fails, he may easily rationalize his failure in terms of having extended his best effort and will probably be upset for a few days, but will quickly recover and be able to do his job without suffering further from the incident.

A Rescuer is a man untrained in the art of lifesaving. While walking down the beach he sees a person drowning, jumps into the surf, and swims out to the victim who, flailing desperately, grabs him so that eventually they both drown.

A person who proposes to be a therapist for alcoholics is a professional rescuer with certain skills, and who is aware of his limitations. If he is a good therapist he will succeed in rescuing most of his patients, although he will always have the very unpleasant experience of failing in some cases. When he fails, he knows that he applied all of his skill in as competent a manner as possible, and will only be affected by the failure temporarily. On the other hand, a therapist who is a game Rescuer without proper understanding of the difficulties that he is dealing with, will rush in to attempt to rescue an alcoholic from irreparable situations, becoming implicated emotionally in such a manner that he will actually find himself drained of confidence and energy. Therapists who accumulate a caseload of patients with whom they are playing the Rescuer may become prey to depression and thoughts of suicide.*

The dramatic reversal or *peripateia* which, according to Aristotle, is one of the requirements of good tragedy, is vividly illustrated by the professional rescuer who becomes a victim of his patients. Karpman has elucidated the mechanics of the dramatic shift of roles which occurs in games and scripts.[27] He postulates that only three roles are necessary to depict the emotional reversals of a tragic drama: the Persecutor, the Rescuer, and the Victim. The situation in which a Rescuer is lulled by seeming success then suddenly finds himself the Victim of his Victim-turned-Persecutor, is often en-

*It is not unlikely that the extremely high incidence of suicide among psychiatrists is due to the process suggested above.

countered by psychotherapists working with hamartic patients. Victimization by one's patients usually occurs in the form of an early morning telephone call from a patient threatening suicide, homicide or some other form of mayhem, for which the therapist can feel some responsibility. A psychotherapist is sometimes held responsible by society for his patient's actions and must therefore remain alert to his patient's potential for mayhem so as not to be taken by surprise. The important thing to remember, once again, is that the payoff of alcoholism, suicide, and other self-destructive behavior is the effect of this behavior on others. The effect that the alcoholic as Victim wishes to have on the psychotherapist as Rescuer is a reaction of dismay and sudden terror. A patient who knows that his therapist will be neither dismayed nor terrorized has no incentive to perform that act. Conversely, a therapist who allows himself to be lulled into a false sense of security by his Child's wish to be an omnipotent Rescuer is, in effect, instigating and provoking self-destructive behavior from the patient. The patient's Child will not be able to resist the temptation to do something self-destructive for the pleasure of observing the therapist's sudden fall from his exalted position as a Rescuer to the pathetic and terror-struck position of Victim. The general antithesis for a professional rescuer is to remain completely aloof from the patient, a technique justifiable in terms of psychoanalytic thinking as a means of fostering transference and avoiding countertransference—i.e., the patient reacting to the therapist as to a mother or father rather than the therapist reacting as a father or mother to the patient. A therapist who remains completely uninvolved will probably not have an opportunity to play Rescuer, but during the counterscript periods of the alcoholic's script, he may have strong rescue fantasies about his effectiveness as a therapist, even though he is not overtly behaving as Rescuer. Therapists who have such fantasies after a dramatic relapse in the patient's behavior, often find themselves in the role of the Persecutor, bitterly resenting what they feel to be the patient's "lack of motivation," "resistance," and "passive-aggressiveness." One notorious Rescue role that I have encountered on occasion, especially with alcoholics of the "Lush" variety, is the one in which the Rescuer's fantasy provokes him into establishing a sexual relationship with the alcoholic, a relationship which he sees as having therapeutic potential. Should a therapist consider his sexual involvements potentially therapeutic, he will probably become involved in an extremely hard game which can be expected to end with a hard payoff. Occasionally, the payoff involves a shift in which the Victim or It becomes Persecutor, and the Rescuer becomes a victim in a court of law. In lesser cases, the persecution may be indignant discussion at social gatherings of the therapist's seduction of the patient, or even just the threat of such discussions.

PATSY

The role of Patsy in the game of "Alcoholic" is usually played by a therapist who hopes to avoid the role of Rescuer in the game. The therapeutic Patsy is a therapist who becomes so involved in theoretical considerations about the origin of drinking, transference and countertransference, unconditional positive regard, resistance, and interpretation of dreams, that he fails to notice the obvious, common-sense dimensions of the problem he is dealing with. One patient described the role aptly: "I've had many therapists, every one of them a sweetheart. Warm, understanding, considerate, but do you realize that in the last twenty years and seven therapists, not one of those boobs asked me to stop drinking?" Alcoholic patients take great delight in noticing the credibility gap that exists in their therapist's behavior and often gleefully describe these gross incongruences at AA meetings and bars.

The credibility gap refers to any situation in which the awareness of the patient and the therapist differs markedly. One instance of this exists if the alcoholic is drinking between therapy meetings, or worse, if he is drunk during meetings without the therapist's knowledge: to the alcoholic this therapist is a Patsy. Similarly, a credibility gap exists if a therapist's awareness is focused on the patient's wish to become pregnant by him, or on his latent homosexual impulses, while the patient merely is aware of being angry at the therapist: in this instance, the therapist is a Patsy to the D&P player, and to the Lush he is a wise, inscrutable Rescuer.

The therapist must be in touch with the real world. He must know the symptoms of drinking, of hangovers, and the alcoholic's ploys and ways of going undetected, and he should stay in touch with his family, friends, and employer. The therapist should always check his interpretations with his patient. Often a patient who has been given a conclusion such as, "I believe that you wanted to have intercourse with your mother," preserves the credibility gap by answering, "I guess you are right, Doc, unconsciously," which is another way of saying either, "Gee, you are wonderful, professor, I don't understand a word you said but I know you'll rescue and take care of me," or, "Wow, this shrink is really out of it, but I'll humor him, who knows, he might come in handy sometime." Such superficial acceptance of interpretations is clear indication that the therapist is playing Patsy or Rescuer. An interpretation is truly accepted only if it is understood and consciously believed by the Adult in the patient.

Another form of Patsy is the therapist who believes that an alcoholic can be cured or even helped solely by whatever transpires in the therapeutic hour. This therapist usually feels that insight or emotional catharsis alone is capable of effecting a cure. Therefore, he allows the patient to avoid responsibility for his situation between meetings and accepts a situation in which the alcoholic is essentially saying, meeting after meeting, "O.K., Doc, here we go again, let's see what you can come up with this time." An easy maneuver against this kind of situation is to assign the patient homework. This will demonstrate within a week whether the patient takes the therapist seriously. Assigning homework is also an antithesis for the situation in which the patient avoids responsibility while thinking of the therapist as a Rescuer. Here the patient who attends meeting after meeting, his heart filled with hope and admiration for the therapist, is being served notice that once again responsibility for his situation lies with him and that the therapeutic hour must be supplemented by work between meetings.

Finally, a therapist who indiscriminately accepts his patient's assurances that he has given up drinking forever, or that he is truly recovered or cured, may be in danger of being a Patsy as well. Accepting such assurances without evidence other than the patient's word is a mistake often committed by novice therapists mostly because they are either overly impressed with their own effectiveness (Rescuer) or because they do not wish to offend the patient with their doubts which they rightly see as being a Persecutor's role. Here, the sophisticated therapist will take a strong, unprejudiced, forthright view, roughly as follows: "I am glad that you are feeling good about yourself, John. If you keep feeling this way for a while, you may have fulfilled your contract," or, in other words, "Let's wait and see."

CONNECTION

The Connection is the ancillary professional who is the source of supply for the alcoholic, and who is in the game for his own profit.

The role of Connection is seldom played by the

psychotherapist although at times the therapist will play the "Alcoholic" game by giving the patient money, or providing services beyond those which have been contracted for, such as driving him about or providing food and shelter. Strictly speaking, however, this is not an example of a Connection but rather of a Patsy who is being conned by the alcoholic.

Physicians who provide drugs which are basically alcohol substitutes may be playing the role of Connection. It is, however, important to distinguish between the physician who provides drugs while in the Rescuing role in an effort to help the patient through a crisis, and the physician whose practice consists of administering drugs to alcoholics and who is not playing the Rescue role but simply making a living by providing drugs, as does the bartender or the drug pusher.

It

A very few psychotherapists are themselves alcoholics, and it is unlikely that they can perform adequate therapy. Yet, theoretically, an alcoholic therapist does not need to play the "Alcoholic" game with his alcoholic patient. The alcoholic therapist would be playing the game with the patient if he caused the patient to take the Rescuing, Persecuting, or Connection role. Thus, if the alcoholic therapist calls his alcoholic patient in order to talk about his problems, he is setting up a game in which he is playing It and the patient is playing Rescuer. Needless to say, this situation is uncommon but by no means unheard of. Playing any of the roles of the alcoholic game is what psychoanalysts call countertransference. The therapist who finds himself playing the game of "Alcoholic" must, in good conscience, bring the situation to an end or transfer his patient to another therapist, since it is quite impossible for a patient to recover from alcoholism as long as his therapist is playing the game with him.

The Gallows Transaction

One additional transaction to be avoided is the gallows transaction, which takes place when It, in one way or another, cons the group members (and sometimes the therapist) into smiling at his script behavior. In hamartic individuals, self-destructive behavior is always associated with a smile. The person who explains the smile by saying, "I'm smiling because it's funny," or "I'm smiling in order not to cry," is falling prey to the Professor's sophistry. A smile is associated with pleasure or more precisely, just as it is in the infant, with deep, physiological well-being. The pleasure in this case is the result of the protection and smile of witch mother or ogre that is awarded for self-destructive behavior. The smile of the therapist or the audience parallels and reinforces the smile of the witch mother or the ogre, who is pleased when It obeys the injunction. For instance, White may come to the group and say, "I got drunk last night, ha, ha," and the therapist or another group member responds, "Sorry to hear that, ha, ha." The verbal content is Adult-to-Adult and the "ha-ha's" are from Child-to-Child or from Child-to-Parent and from Parent-to-Child. The patient's smile is primarily addressed to the witch mother or ogre. The Child learns by conditioning and is stimulus-bound, so that the smile of the respondent serves to reinforce the Child's self-destructive behavior. A therapist dealing with self-destructive individuals must determine which behavior is self-destructive or script-bound, and must never smile in response to it. When the gallows transaction is explained in a group and is thus prevented from occurring, the effect on the patient is startling, and often his Child reacts as if the therapist is a party-crasher who made away with the goodies. Curtailing the gallows transaction does not mean that therapy should not be fun, but simply that self-destruction is no fun. In the discussion of therapeutic tissue-responses, fun will be explored as one of the essential moves in therapy. Avoiding the gallows transaction allows the group to laugh at whatever is joyful rather than tragic in the patient, and discourages the self-destructive aspects of his behavior by denying the strokes he expects, and usually gets for it.

CHAPTER SEVENTEEN

Treatment Strategies in Script Analysis

AVOIDANCE OF role playing by the therapist, which is intuitively understood by psychoanalytic and nondirective therapists, has caused the type of therapeutic activity in which the therapist hides behind a mask of noncommittal passivity while the patient thrashes about in discomfort.

By retaining a strictly noncommittal Adult-to-Adult relationship, psychotherapists have rejected the kind of behavior which is essential to the therapy of hamartic scripts. All the roles of the game of "Alcoholic" are played from either a Parent or Child ego state and require what may be called "tissue" or "gut" responses. By rejecting all tissue responses, therapists have thrown out the baby with the bathwater, so to speak, since tissue responses are needed for the effective treatment of scripts. By making it possible to dissect minutely the possible transactions between the therapist and patient, transactional analysis gives the therapist a number of therapeutic strategies, in addition to Adult-to-Adult work, which are needed to treat patients with tissue-destructive scripts. These strategies, outlined in the following discussion, involve the therapist's Parent and Child ego states, but are not Rescuing, Persecuting, or Patsy-like transactions.

WORK

The Work transaction (Figure 6A) is most common among "rational" and "insight" therapists. It represents Adult-to-Adult communication in which 1) data is gathered—the patient's life history, his drinking patterns, childhood or recent events in his life, his dreams; 2) conclusions are drawn—interpretation of dreams, diagnosis of ego states and games, interpretation of resistances; and 3) recommendations are made which are Adult statements of logical consequences or predictions such as "Well, given what you've told me, it would seem that you are no longer able to control your drinking," or "It appears that you are working too hard; if you reduce your working schedule, you might not feel the urge to drink at the end of the day."

Work transactions represent the largest percentage of transactions occurring in group treatment and take a certain predictable course. Work tends to be carried out with one group member as the focus. Either by his own choosing or by being singled out by someone else, one group member will become the center of attention. This does not necessarily mean that he will be placed on the "hot seat" where he becomes the focus of all interaction but simply that he tends to be at the center of it. The first phase of this process is one of *clarification*. The patient presents a problem or someone else suggests that a problem exists, and some exploration is needed to ascertain whether there is in reality something to work on. The problem suggested by the patient may be a "red herring" or a "bone" thrown at the group to distract it from a more serious problem. Or the problem, suggested by another group member, may represent a projection or misperception about the patient. In any case, the process of clarification continues

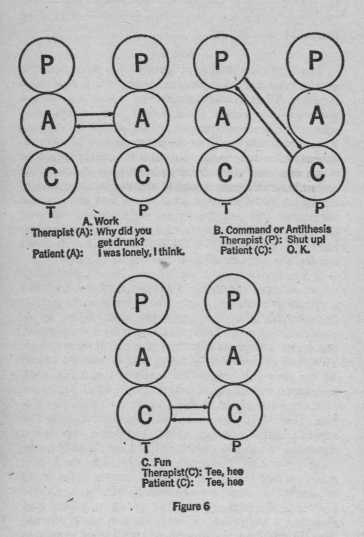

A. Work
Therapist (A): Why did you get drunk?
Patient (A): I was lonely, I think.

B. Command or Antithesis
Therapist (P): Shut up!
Patient (C): O. K.

C. Fun
Therapist (C): Tee, hee
Patient (C): Tee, hee

Figure 6

until the feeling develops that the group is working on a real problem area in which some change can or should occur. At this point, the process shifts from clarification to *challenge* and someone will ask, overtly or covertly, "Now that you know the problem, what are you going to do about it?" The patient ordinarily is at a loss for solutions or unwilling to use those which are suggested. A cherished old pattern of behavior is being re-examined, a parental injunction is being challenged, and the patient's Adapted Child is expected to balk. This is the *sick point* or *impasse* beyond which the patient will not go unless pressure is applied, pressure which can only come from another person's Child or Parent.[34] At this point, a purely Work-oriented therapist has to rely on one of the group members to supply the tissue transactions needed. The transactional analyst, however, has at his disposal the Permission transaction and will use it when appropriate. At this point the process shifts from challenge to *climax* if the patient accepts the Permission, or to *anticlimax* if he deflects it. If Permission is accepted, the group members will ordinarily have an experience of well-being and closure, and a silence will follow after which the process starts anew with another patient as the focus of attention. If the behavior for which Permission was given occurs within the group itself, such as getting angry, crying, being honest, etc., the patient may be quite shaken and Protection may be indicated.

If the patient deflects the Permission, the therapist is faced with a question of strategy. Should he continue to press the patient or should he give up and go on to someone else? This is probably the most crucial decision in group treatment. The therapist who is under time pressure has the dual responsibility of not allowing time to be wasted and of pursuing matters to their completion. Skillful decisions along these lines distinguish the experienced therapist from the novice who will either pursue matters endlessly to no avail or drop them just as the impasse is ready to be broken. In any case, if the matter is dropped, the feeling in the group is anticlimactic and again a silence follows, after which a new person becomes the focus of attention.

ANTITHESIS OR COMMAND

This is an emergency transaction from Parent to Child which is used to arrest or interfere with certain transactional sequences deemed undesirable by the therapist (Figure 6B). For instance, if two patients in a group are engaging in a flirtation which may lead to a sexual association, he may arbitrarily say to one, Parent to Child, "I don't think you should get together with Mary outside of the group." Or, if an intoxicated patient in the group continually interrupts the proceedings, the therapist might say, again Parent to Child, "Shut up!" This transaction has to be available to a therapist dealing with patients who have hamartic scripts, since these patients are sometimes disruptive and require direct commands.

I have seen dramatic evidence of the effectiveness of the Antithesis transaction with self-destructive individuals. It has become routine to use a script Antithesis such as "Don't kill yourself," or "Don't beat your children" with suicidal or violent patients. These patients have often reported hearing the therapist's voice and injunction whenever tempted to kill themselves or to beat their children. These patients often express their appreciation for the positive effect of the therapist's injunction without which, they feel, they might have committed a suicidal or violent act.

FUN

Fun is a transaction in which the Child of the therapist and the Child of the patient are able to experience joy together (Figure 6C). This transaction is often confused with its destructive counterpart, the gallows transaction, and is therefore avoided by some experienced therapists because they fear its possible dangers. Yet Child-to-Child fun seems to be a basic requirement of efficient therapy, and while a therapist may cure a patient without having any fun, the cure is likely to be more speedy if they are having fun together. Fun also has the advantage of making the therapist's task more enjoyable, something which is of benefit to the patient since a zestful, happy therapist is likely to have fewer days out of work from sickness, and less interference by depression than a therapist who is not having fun in his work.

Fun is most readily expressed through laughter. Because of this, a group member or a therapist who doesn't laugh heartily at least once per meeting should consider seriously whether he is not being unnecessarily glum.

PERMISSION

One of the three P's of transactional analysis treatment (Permission, Protection, Potency), Permission is a transaction which is intimately tied to the theory of scripts (Figure 7A). One occasionally hears therapists saying that an alcoholic needs permission to drink without guilt. The implication here is that it is because of his neurotic guilt about drinking that the drinking continues. Transactional analysis takes the superficially surprising view that an alcoholic needs permission *not* to drink, because he is under duress to do so. This concept loses its surprising aspects if one remembers that an alcoholic is involved in a script, and that a script is the result of parental injunctions. As a consequence, theoretically, the alcoholic is under orders to drink, and needs permission not to. The concept of Permission becomes very clear when applied, for example, to a young alcoholic who is surrounded by hard-drinking co-workers, and who would feel a loss of self-esteem if he decided that drinking is harmful to him, and should be discontinued. This person would

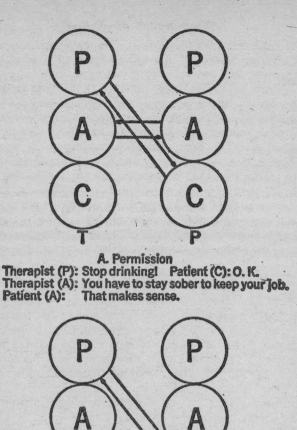

A. Permission
Therapist (P): Stop drinking!   Patient (C): O. K.
Therapist (A): You have to stay sober to keep your job.
Patient (A):   That makes sense.

B. Protection
Patient (C):.   I am scared
Therapist (P): Don't worry,
everything will be O. K.

Figure 7

clearly need permission to stop drinking and go against the covert and often even overt challenges of his co-workers to continue drinking.

Similarly, though perhaps not as obviously, every alcoholic patient needs permission not to drink, or permission to see his drinking as the cause of his difficulties rather than a remedy for them—as most alcoholics see it (occasionally with the help of misinformed professionals who view alcoholism as a defense against psychosis).

Permission, then, is a transaction in which the therapist attempts to align the patient with his original script-free, Natural Child ego state. In the case of the alcoholic, this ego state is one in which self-preservation takes precedence over parental injunctions. The Permission transaction is a combination of a Parent-to-Child command, as described above—"Stop drinking" —and a rational, logical explanation, Adult-to-Adult, in which the rational or logical reason for the command is explained ("You will not regain your job unless you stop drinking," etc.).

Permission requires the involvement of the patient's Adult, and if his Adult is not convinced that the therapist's Adult statement is valid, Permission simply becomes a Command that may be resisted by the patient. It is possible that decontamination of the patient's Adult will be needed. For instance, the patient who is about to lose his job because he drinks may ignore the statement "You will not regain your job unless you stop drinking," because he believes that he will not regain his job unless he can drink socially. Thus, if the Adult-to-Adult message is not received and accepted, Permission will not work. The therapeutic task at this point would be to recognize the contamination involved, namely, that the patient believes that he has to drink in order to keep his job.

The two fundamental injunctions most alcoholics need Permission against are not to discuss their parents and not to discuss themselves in the group. When these injunctions exist, very little therapy can take place until they are overcome, and dealing with them should therefore constitute the first order of business.

Offering Antabuse is the most succinct and elegant from of Permission in the therapy of alcoholics. When Antabuse is accepted by the patient's Child from the therapist's Parent, and when the patient's Adult understands taking Antabuse as "making sense," then the situation constitutes Permission to stop drinking. If the Antabuse is accepted only by the Child, it constitutes an Antithesis or temporary moratorium on the life course, since without Adult recognition of the validity of complete cessation of drinking, the patient will eventually start drinking again. Patients whose Child is not willing to accept the Parental command from the therapist will not ingest the Antabuse, even if the Adult sees that taking it makes sense. Thus, a patient whose Adult recognizes that he must stop drinking to get better, but whose Child is unwilling to accept the therapist's Parental command, usually says something like "Yes, doctor, I know I should stop drinking but I would rather do it myself."

The use of Permission as a therapeutic maneuver does not end with the achievement of sobriety. The sober alcoholic is generally still under one or more paralyzing injunctions from his parents. He may not have permission to think, talk, move, demand, laugh, cry, or to give and take, accept and reject strokes. As therapy progresses during sobriety the patient will improve along some lines but will often refuse to take action along other lines essential to his permanent improvement. For instance, an alcoholic patient who had very visibly improved her situation by remaining sober for a whole year never initiated social relationships herself, but rather relied for her social contacts on whatever activities her few friends initiated. When this was noticed it became evident that she needed Permission to make demands from people. She was told, as part of her homework, to call someone and ask them to a movie. This proved to be a very difficult task for her, and she was not able to perform it for a few weeks. This difficulty became the focus of the therapy, the patient's *sick point* beyond which she had to move in order to proceed toward permanent improvement. The therapist's insistence and interest in this specific action eventually had the desired effect and she finally overthrew the strong injunction against making demands of people, an act which proved to be crucial in her eventual cure.

It must be remembered that the Parent giving Permission should be the grownup Parent (P_2), and not the Parent in the Child $(P_1$ in $C_2)$ (see Figure 2). The difference between the first-order Parent and the Parent in the Child has been elaborated in the first chapter, but it should be noted that the Parent in the Child plays the part of impotent Rescuer or Persecutor in the game of Alcoholic. The potency required to countermand parental injunctions is not available to the Parent in the Child but only to the first-order Parent. Every therapist should be aware of the difference between these two ego states in himself, since any transactions coming from the Parent in the Child of the therapist are always an indication of difficulty.

PROTECTION

The concept of therapeutic protection was first postulated by Patricia Crossman and has become an indispensable part of transactional analysis treatment.[11] When a patient, under the influence of the therapist's Permission, takes a step which involves rejection of the parental injunction, he may find himself alone and terrified, having declined parental protection. The existential vacuum and fear that follows cannot be ignored by the therapist. If the therapist does not replace the Protection that the patient has lost from his parents

(Figure 7B), the patient will probably return to his prior mode of behavior within which he feels safe, and allow the witch mother or ogre to "return." This constitutes a re-embracement of the script and, psychologically speaking, it represents the patient's belief that the therapist is not as powerful as the witch or orge and that he cannot be trusted when "the chips are down."

Because the patient has to rely on the therapist's Protection, the timing of Permissions is important. They should be given only when both the therapist and patient feel that Protection is possible. Thus, they should not be given before going on vacation, or when schedules are likely to be overcrowded. The need for Protection may arise at almost any time; therapists who prefer to isolate themselves from their patients may fail to be available for Protection when needed. Protection is often provided over the telephone, since the panic that follows Permission does not always coincide with therapeutic appointments. Experience shows that, with a caseload of about fifty patients, a therapist will need to provide Protection about twice a week outside of the regularly scheduled appointments. I have made my home telephone available to all of my patients and have encountered very little difficulty because of it. By remembering that any "distress" phone call may be either an invitation to play Rescuer over the phone or a genuine call for Protection, it is relatively simple to separate the "game" phone calls from the calls for Protection. In general, a genuine call for Protection takes less than fifteen minutes and is a highly satisfying experience for both the therapist and the patient. An invitation to play Rescuer has a totally different feel to it since whatever the therapist says to reassure the patient is received with a "Yes, but," which is simply a further invitation for another move within the Rescue role. When a patient calls and is clearly attempting to hook the therapist into a Rescue role, the therapist should quickly decline any further conversation and remind the patient of the responsibility for his own actions. Consider the following conversation:

Patient: Hello.
Therapist: Hello.
Patient (*crying*): I'm scared.
Therapist: What's the matter?
Patient: I don't know, I'm scared and I feel like drinking.
Therapist: I understand. It's pretty scary to try to do things differently from what your script calls for. I suggest that you call up a friend and go to a movie tonight.
Patient: That sounds like a good idea. I think I'll do it.
Therapist: That's good, hang on tight, and feel free to call me anytime you get scared again.
Patient: I feel better now. Thank you.
Therapist: Goodbye.
Patient: Goodbye.

The above conversation is a typical Protection transaction. Notice that the patient is willing to accept responsibility for his emotional state, and is willing to accept the therapist's recommendations to change it. The patient is genuinely scared and responds in a favorable manner in a relatively short period of time. Consider in contrast the following conversation:

Patient: Hello.
Therapist: Hello.
Patient (*crying*): I'm scared.
Therapist: What's the matter?
Patient: I haven't had a drink for ten days, and I feel like getting drunk.
Therapist: I understand how you feel. It's pretty scary to try to do things differently from what your script calls for. I suggest that you call up a friend and go to a movie tonight.
Patient: I don't feel like doing that. I don't have any friends. Can't you do better than that? If you can't do better than that, I think I'm going to get drunk.
Therapist: What would you like me to do?

Patient: I want you to talk to me, or give me some medication, or something.
Therapist: What are you going to do about the situation?
Patient: I don't know, I think I'll get drunk.
Therapist: Well, I hope you won't, but I don't exactly understand what you want me to do. I suggest that you get out of the house and go to a movie.
Patient: Yes, but . . . , etc.

The above conversation is a clear attempt on the part of the patient to draw the therapist into a Rescue role. If the therapist is willing, this conversation can go on for hours and have essentially no results. If the therapist is unwilling to cooperate, the patient may decide to abandon the attempt. If he does, he is much less likely to think of the therapist as a possible Rescuer and will probably not repeat the attempt in the future. Occasionally a patient will call after getting drunk and a conversation under those circumstances is totally useless and should be politely declined until the patient sobers up.

Protection is akin to what is commonly known as "supportive" treatment, except that in transactional analysis it is seen as a temporary necessity following Permission rather than as a treatment approach applied to certain borderline or psychotic patients. Supportive treatment ordinarily implies that the therapist considers the patient unable to change in any meaningful way. Protection simply means that the therapist recognizes that the patient, having broken the impasse, will be in a temporary state of anxiety and existential vacuum. Protection also needs to be distinguished from a "transference cure" in which the patient's improvement is predicated on a continuing involvement with the therapist. Ordinarily, a patient does not require protection for more than three months following abandonment of the script. If the patient's panic and need for the therapist do not subside by that time, the therapist is probably playing Rescuer in the patient's game.

THERAPEUTIC POTENCY

These four tissue transactions, in addition to the Adult-to-Adult transaction, constitute the transactional analyst's basic tools. Adding Antithesis, Fun, Permission, and Protection to the Work transaction gives the transactional analyst flexibility and latitude and provides him with increased therapeutic effectiveness or Potency. Therapeutic Potency refers to the therapist's capacity to bring about a speedy cure. The Potency of the therapist has to be commensurate with the potency of the injunction laid down by the parents of the patient, and it is an attribute which transactional analysts seek in their work. Potency implies that the therapist is willing to attempt to cure the patient, to permit himself to do so, and to estimate the time and expense involved. It means that he is willing to confront the patient at the *impasse* or sick point and to exert pressure, and it means that the therapist is willing to provide Protection for the patient when it is needed. Potency, when striven for by therapists, is often interpreted as implying a wish for omnipotence. However, the difference between Potency and omnipotence is quite clear, and transactional analysts, aware of their limitations as well as those of the concept of therapeutic Potency, are seldom plagued by the countertransference phenomenon called "fantasies of omnipotence" or, in transactional terms, by being hooked into the Rescuer role.

The desirability of therapeutic Potency makes transactional analysts willing to consider for use any technique which demonstrably accelerates treatment. Techniques which contribute to a speedy cure are Permission classes, Marathons, and Homework.

1) *Permission Classes.* Group treatment sessions have their limitations as therapeutic tools. They are arranged primarily for the purpose of verbal interaction among ten or fewer individuals and they tend to take place in a room of limited size. In addition, time is limited and

the fees paid to the therapist are generally high. Many professional therapists feel that they are bound by their ethical code to sharply limit their physical contact with their patients.

Transactional analysts have amplified the potency of group treatment by referring their patients to Permission classes led by a Permission teacher.[40] These classes are recommended to selected patients whose parental injunctions inhibit them not only in their thinking and talking (which can be dealt with in group treatment), but also in more physical ways, such as in touching and being able to be touched; moving in an expansive, graceful or assertive way; laughing or crying; dancing or cutting up; moving sexually or aggressively; relaxing; and so on.

Permission classes preferably meet at a dance studio with mirrors on the wall and soft mats available for the floor. Each patient is referred to the Permission class with a specific prescription such as "Permission to dance," "Permission to touch others," "Permission to be sexy," "Permission to act assertively," or "Permission to lead instead of follow," to mention a few.

The Permission teacher, not necessarily a trained psychotherapist, but trained in dance, body awareness, body movement, improvisation, role playing, and aware of structural analysis, meets with a group of eight to twelve patients for about two hours weekly. The patients are free to communicate with the Permission teacher on whatever subject they desire, but the therapist and the Permission teacher do not necessarily discuss their cases, except insofar as the Permission prescriptions need to be clarified.

While most patients can enjoy Permission classes, not all need them. Thus, they are not prescribed for all patients nor are they prescribed for any patient in whom it is not clear what Permission is needed.

2) *Marathons*. Marathons, or protracted therapy meetings lasting between twelve and thirty-six hours,

are another technique which amplifies therapeutic Potency. I have found Marathons extremely useful for patients who, after several months of therapy, have arrived at an impasse or sick point beyond which they seem unable to move. Patients who are on an improvement plateau in treatment and who have not made any recent progress are selected for participation in a Marathon. Typically, the session begins with a discussion of the goals each patient hopes to achieve during the Marathon. These goals are written on a large sheet of paper or on the wall to be clearly visible to all the members participating,* and work toward achieving these goals continues throughout the period of the Marathon.

The success of these sessions is unquestionable; patients are usually quite elated and feel a great sense of accomplishment and satisfaction at the end of a Marathon, a sense of euphoria which usually lasts from one to two weeks. This sense of euphoria eventually abates and is often followed by a slight depression. It is therefore very important that during the two or three weeks following the session, the therapist and the patient concentrate on securing the gains made during the Marathon. As an example, a young man who attends a Marathon for the purpose of "being assertive" might become quite assertive during the session and feel strong and masterful as he leaves the meeting. If, in the next two weeks, he does not repeatedly apply his new-gained confidence, he will lose it. Thus, Marathons require follow-up without which their accomplishments are often deceptive and short-lived.

3) *Homework.* Homework is assigned work that the patient does between therapy meetings toward the fulfillment of his contract. Often patients will do homework without any urging from the therapist or the group. It is not unlikely that it is those patients who profit from

---

*Dr. Franklin Ernst was the first to utilize wall markings or graffiti as a technique which improves therapeutic effectiveness.[15]

"insight" therapies in which much emphasis is placed on what transpires during the therapeutic hour. A patient who generates his own homework is likely to assume responsibility for his situation and assume that he must do something about it. I pointed out earlier that all the diagnostic labels or categories heretofore applied to alcoholics seem to make very little, if any, sense. Based on the concept of homework, however, one valuable diagnostic label seems to emerge: workers versus nonworkers. The latter category is not to be confused with the familiar term, "unmotivated." Many patients who would be called motivated, because they attend regularly, pay fees, participate in the group, are nonworkers. The concept of motivation is hypothetical: a worker, on the other hand, is a person who uses suggestions given him by the therapist or group members and tries them out, discarding those that do not work and keeping those that do. Whether a person is a worker or not is the best prognostic tool known to me. Workers who seemed to other therapists to be hopelessly psychotic have achieved their goals within a year of group treatment, while nonworkers with minor neurotic symptoms have made little change in two years.

The kinds of homework assigned are as varied as the symptoms they are intended to counteract. A large segment of homework assignments is devised to overcome social anxiety by systematic desensitization, an approach borrowed from behavior therapy. A shy patient, for example, is given increasingly difficult social tasks starting with one he find simple to perform. Beginning with such things as asking the time of day on a busy street, the homework includes a number of items, each one to be performed repeatedly. Each homework assignment is more difficult than the last one: asking the time of day, then asking for elaborate directions; smiling at people in the street, then complimenting someone on his appearance; making small talk, and so on. The purpose is to teach the patient how to obtain strokes. Another type of homework is assertion with significant persons. A patient's homework may be to ask his boss for a raise, to tell his wife that from now on he will take a night out, to tell his mother-in-law to move out, or to call a woman he likes and ask her for a date. The conversations involved are often rehearsed in group, and this procedure—as well as the whole activity of devising and assigning homework—is often the source of much fun.

A person who suffers from a contamination of the Adult such as "I am no good," "Everyone who says that they like me is lying to make me feel better," "The people in this group are communist agents," may be asked to write an essay defending the opposite point of view: "I am a good man," "People love me and like me," "The people in this group are just patients like myself." One woman who called herself a monster was asked to draw a picture of it because she had no words to describe it. Having done this, she was able to realize what a distorted and unreasonable view she had of herself.

Other forms of homework such as following a tight schedule of activities, having fun, and looking up old friends are assigned to teach patients how to structure time to replace an abandoned game.

When homework is assigned, it is important to check on it the following week. If the therapist forgets the assignment, he takes the risk that neither the patient nor the group will bring it up, and this will surely put him in the Patsy role with the patient. If the patient did not do his homework it is reassigned, and if this reoccurs his sincerity is challenged. Often a patient finds the assignment too difficult and the homework has to be redesigned to fit his present capacities.

4) *Touching.* Touching patients is a therapeutic maneuver of great potency which has fallen into disrepute, probably because of the dangers associated with it. As in the example of laughter where Fun is thera-

peutic and the gallows transaction is harmful, the use of touch with patients needs to be thoroughly explored and its therapeutical potential isolated from its harmful possibilities. Touch is the most basic tissue transaction and there is evidence that it is an essential ingredient in the cure of schizophrenia.[36] In my opinion, physical strokes are a specific and powerful antidote to depression, except in the rare cases where it is clearly related to organic causes. Chronic depression is almost always caused by stroke deprivation, and cured when the patient obtains constant and adequate stroking.

Based on the above consideration, it seems prudent at this time, due to a lack of clear understanding about the negative effects of touching, to handle this potent therapeutic tool with care. I encourage a minimum of touching between therapist and patient, and a maximum of touching between patients within the treatment session, while discouraging social contact between therapist and patient and intimate contact between patients outside of treatment sessions.

These auxiliary techniques of group treatment amplify the therapeutic Potency of the transactional analyst. Clearly, as therapists experiment with new techniques and creative practitioners explore the vast array of possibilities which may increase their effectiveness, other approaches will be added to the tried and tested approaches available today.*

One extremely fertile source of such approaches is the Esalen Institute in Big Sur, California, where the exploration of human potentialities ranges from Awareness and Encounter through Positive Disintegration, Reincarnation and Karma, all the way to Zen Meditation.[16]

---

*In order to avoid experimenting with little-understood methods with patients who justifiably expect a therapist to treat them rather than experiment, on occasion I have organized groups called "Laboratories in Group Dynamics." These groups are clearly specified not to be therapeutic groups, but laboratories in which each person participates at his own risk. They have proven extremely valuable in exploring unusual approaches which, after proper evaluation, can be used with patients in their treatment.

Summary

TRANSACTIONAL ANALYSIS is a new technique of psychotherapy, based on the writings of Eric Berne, which has been used for the modification of behavior since approximately 1958. It is an original and sophisticated theory of personality as well as a distinct technical departure from currently held views of psychotherapy.

The foundation of the transactional theory of personality is based on three major concepts: ego states, games, and scripts. A person's behavior is described in terms of three observable ego states which are modalities of the individual's ego. The ego here is understood as defined by psychoanalytic ego theorists from Freud to Erikson. Not to be confused with ego, super-ego, and id, ego states are modes of ego activity, each one uniquely adapted to different types of situations. The mode of the Child is behavior remnant from childhood, adapted to creative and pleasurable activities; the Adult mode is dispassionate behavior, adapted to rational, logical, and scientific thought; and the Parent mode is a reproduction of the behavior of one or more parental figures, adapted to nurturing and to making judgments when sufficient data is unavailable. A person's ego is assumed to operate in one and only one of these modalities at any one time.

Any relationship between two or more people can be diagrammed as transactions between ego states. A game is the most common disturbance of observable behavior, and is defined as a series of transactions with a covert motive and a payoff. The importance of games lies primarily in the fact that they are the medium by which a person obtains strokes, and that a succession of games played end to end is necessary for the consummation of a script.

Transactional analysts regard all psychopathology, with the exception of some organically caused forms, as transactional disturbances understandable in terms of the covert motivation of the individual's Child. Because of their belief that pathology is primarily the result of external interaction, transactional analysts regard psychiatric adjectives which are addressed to hypothetical internal states—such as passive, anxious, manipulative, hostile, neurotic, schizoid, character disordered, and so on—with the suspicion that the covert purpose of these words is primarily to insult, control, or dismiss the persons to whom these terms are applied.

The script is a consciously understood life plan, usually decided upon before the age of fourteen, and psychopathologies, such as alcoholism, depression, schizophrenia, homosexuality, etc., often represent a script, that is, they are the result of consciously made childhood decisions. Each of these decisions is an adaptation by the young person to the realities and pressures of his childhood situation, adaptive and synthetic maneuvers of the child's ego which may remain as guideposts for the person's behavior until his death.

Transactional analysis is a technique of treatment that has the following unique features.

LANGUAGE

The language of transactional analysis is designed to to both understandable and attractive to most individuals seeking psychotherapy. The reason for the use of such colloquialisms as Child, game, racket, and trading stamps, is grounded in the conviction that the language used by the therapist to understand his patient should be maximally understandable and minimally polysyllabic, or as simple as possible. It is the intention of the therapist to communicate with the patient on all the aspects of his thinking in regard to treatment, and it is desirable that the patient and the therapist use language which can be understood by both.

RESPONSIBILITY

Responsibility is a key issue in transactional analysis. The patient is considered responsible for his actions because his disturbance is the result of decisions he has made. At the same time, the therapist is considered responsible for his actions toward the patient, and his only legitimate activity as a therapist is the achievement of a speedy cure. A corollary of this position of responsibility is that transactional analysis is a contractual form of treatment in which a patient who is responsible for his actions enters into a contract with a therapist who will attempt to cure or modify permanently a state of affairs which the patient deems undesirable.

GROUP TREATMENT

The ideal context for the treatment of alcoholics is the group, even though individual sessions may be used when needed. The term "group psychotherapy" presently refers to an extremely large and vaguely delineated number of activities, but transactional analysts place certain limits on their definition of the term. 1) Group treatment is seen as requiring a leader who, in a contractual form of treatment, is the therapist. Co-therapists are considered unnecessary and undesirable, unless the co-therapist is a trainee who is there to learn, rather than to share responsibility for treatment. 2) A group contains six to twelve patients, eight ideally, since fewer than six patients is not fertile ground for transactions, and more than eight patients are not likely to be amenable to constant surveillance by the leader. 3) Transactional analysis is primarily a verbal therapy which assumes that behavior can be modified by an exchange of verbal utterances. Physical attack, dance, nudity, are not used within the context of group treatment but, when indicated, a transactional analyst may prescribe some other therapeutic activity for a patient as part of Permission. 4) Selection of patients for groups is seen as unnecessary and undesirable. The ideal group is one which contains people who are different in as many dimensions as possible. Any human being—with the possible exception of the deaf, persons with IQ's lower than 70, or children younger than twelve—is seen as suitable for treatment in the same group, as long as he is able to enter into a contractual relationship involving mutual consent. (This excludes persons who suffer from such conditions as toxic psychosis or chronic brain syndrome, or who are heavily drugged.) The effect of this lack of selectivity is to bring together groups of eight people, rather than groups of eight alcoholics, homosexuals, or schizophrenics. The only time selection is desirable is when a therapist wishes to avoid the constitution of a homogeneous group.*

PERMISSION

Therapeutic Potency requires the therapist to apply every technique which may effectively increase the speed of cure. A minute analysis of the transactions between patient and therapist makes the transactional analyst able to distinguish those transactions likely to harm the patients from those which may be therapeutic. Psychotherapists have tended to limit themselves to the Adult-to-Adult Work transaction, in order to avoid the possible deleterious effects of tissue transactions involving the Parent or the child ego states. By sorting out Parent- and Child-originated transactions which would promote

*For instance, in a clinic for alcoholics where the majority of applicants are male and between the ages of forty and fifty, a therapist is justified in insisting that some younger persons, some women, and patients with problems other than alcoholism be included in the group.

the patient's games and script, transactional analysts are able to use the remaining transactions such as Permission and Protection, among others, for therapeutic purposes.

Permission is a transaction in which the Parent of the therapist directs the patient to perform certain behavior, which the patient's Adult already recognizes as necessary. This transaction occurs in treatment when the patient has reached an impasse beyond which he cannot or will not move. The situation is seen as one in which a patient and a therapist who have previously agreed to work on a certain condition of the patient, confront each other. The patient's resistance to change is seen as the result of his parent's injunction and the subsequent decision. The situation in which the therapist confronts the patient in this manner is called Permission because it involves giving the patient permission to do something he wishes to do, but which is in direct opposition to his parent's wishes. It can be seen, then, that the Permission transaction is one in which the therapist takes a parental, directive role, justified by the previously agreed-to terms of the treatment contract.

PROTECTION

Protection follows logically from Permission. The patient, having taken the therapist's Permission to disobey his parents' injunction, finds himself in a temporary state of panic and existential vacuum during which he needs temporary protection by the therapist.

POTENCY

Permission, Protection, and other Child or Parent transactions which are therapeutic involve behavior on the part of the therapist that is best characterized by the word Potency. Potency is expressed in Permission by the emphasis in which Permission is given, and is exemplified in Protection by the willingness of the therapist to temporarily help carry the burden of the patient's panic. Potency implies that the therapist is willing to attempt to cure the patient, to commit himself to do so, and to estimate the time and expense involved. It implies also that the therapist recognizes the patients for whom other therapists or other approaches might be more effective than his, and that he will search for and add to his techniques those which demonstrably amplify the therapeutic Potency of his approach.

Bibliography

1. Adler, Alfred. *The Individual Psychology of Alfred Adler*. Edited by Heinz L. Ansbacher and Rowena R. Ansbacher. New York: Basic Books, 1956.

2. *Alcoholics Anonymous*. New York: Alcoholic Anonymous Publishing Company, 1955.

3. Aristotle. *Poetics*. New York: The Modern Library, 1954.

4. Bailey, Margaret B., and Stewart, Jean. "Normal Drinking by Persons Reporting Previous Problem Drinking." *Quarterly Journal of Studies on Alcohol* 28,2 (1967): 305–15.

5. Berne, Eric. *Games People Play*. New York: Grove Press, 1964.

6. ———. "Preliminary Orientation ITAA Summer Conference." *Transactional Analysis Bulletin* 5,20 (1966): 171–72.

7. ———. *Principles of Group Treatment*. New York: Oxford University Press, 1966. Also published as *Group Treatment*. New York: Grove Press, An Evergreen Black Cat Book, 1970.

8. ———. *Transactional Analysis in Psychotherapy*. New York: Grove Press, 1961.

9. ———. *The Structure and Dynamics of Organizations and Groups*. New York: J. B. Lippincott, 1963; Grove Press, An Evergreen Book, 1966.

10. Chafetz, Morris E. "The Past Revisited." *International Journal of Psychiatry* 5,1 (1948): 47–48.

11. Crossman, Patricia. "Permission and Protection." *Transactional Analysis Bulletin* 5,19 (1966): 152–53.

12. Donner, Lawrence, and Guerney, Jr., Bernard G.

"Automated Group Dessensitization for Test Anxiety." *Behavioral Research and Therapy* 7,1 (1969): 1–13.

13. Ellis, Albert. *Reason and Emotion in Psychotherapy.* New York: Lyle Stuart, 1962.

14. Erikson, Erik H· *Identity: Youth and Crisis,* New York: W. W. Norton, 1968.

15. Ernst, Franklin. Lecture delivered at the summer conference of the Golden Gate Group Psychotherapy Association, San Francisco, 1968.

16. *Esalen Programs.* Big Sur, California: Esalen Institute Brochure, 1969.

17. Escalona, Sibylle K., and Bergman, Paula. "Unusual Sensitivities in Very Young Children." *Psychoanalytic Study of the Child,* vol. III. New York: International Universities Press, 1949, pp. 333–52.

18. Frank, Jerome D. "The Role of Hope in Psychotherapy." *International Journal of Psychiatry* 5 (1968): 383–95.

19. Franks, Cyril M. "Conditioning and Conditioned Aversion Therapies in the Treatment of the Alcoholic." *International Journal of Addictions* 1 (1966): 61–98.

20. Freud, Sigmund. *The Interpretation of Dreams.* In *The Basic Writings.* New York: Modern Library, 1938.

21. Gitlow, Stanley E. *A Pharmacological Approach to Alcoholism.* New York: Alcoholics Anonymous Grapevine (newsletter), 1968, *See also:* Ditman, Keith S. "No Wonder Drugs for Drinkers." *California Alcoholism Review* 1,3 (1966): 48–52.

22. Goldstein, Arnold P. *Therapist-Patient Expectations in Psychotherapy.* New York: Pergamon Press, 1962.

23. Greenspoon, Joel. "Verbal Conditioning and Clinical Psychology." In *Experimental Foundations of Clinical Psychology,* edited by A. J. Bachrach. New York: Basic Books, 1962.

24. Haley, Jay. *Strategies of Psychotherapy.* New York: Grune and Stratton, 1963.

25. Hartman, Heinz. "Ego Psychology and the Problem of Adaptation." In *Organization and Pathology of Thought,* edited by D. Rapaport. New York: Columbia University Press, 1951.

26. Johnson, Adelaide M., and Szurek, Stanislas A. "The

Genesis of Antisocial Acting Out in Children and Adults." *Psychoanalytic Quarterly* 21 (1952): 323–43.

27. Karpman, Stephen B. "Script Drama Analysis." *Transactional Analysis Bulletin* 7,26*(1968): 39–43.

28. McCord, William, and McCord, Joan. *Origins of Alcoholism.* Stanford, California: Stanford University Press, 1961.

29. *Manual on Alcoholism.* Washington, D.C.: American Medical Association, 1967.

30. Menninger, Karl A. *Man Against Himself.* New York: Harcourt & Brace & Co., 1938.

31. Merton, Robert K. *Social Theory and Social Structure.* Glencoe, Ill.: Free Press, 1957.

32. Nurse, Rodney. Personal communication. 1968.

33. Olivier, Ted. Personal communication. 1967.

34. Perls, Fritz S. *Gestalt Therapy Verbatim.* Lafayette, California: Real People Press, 1969.

35. Piaget, Jean. *Logic and Psychology.* New York: Basic Books, 1957.

36. Schiff, Jacqui L. "Reparenting Schizophrenics." *Transactional Analysis Bulletin* 8,31 (1969): 47–63.

37. Sophocles. *The Oedipus Cycle.* New York: Harcourt Brace and World, 1949.

38. Spitz, Renée. "Hospitalism, Genesis of Psychiatric Conditions in Early Childhood." *Psychoanalytic Study of the Child* 1 (1945): 53–74.

39. Stedman, Thomas Lathorp. *Stedman's Medical Dictionary.* 20th ed. Baltimore: The Williams and Wilkins Co., 1962.

40. Steiner, Claude M., and Steiner, Ursula. "Permission Classes." *Transactional Analysis Bulletin* 7,28 (1968): 89.

41. Werner, Heinz. *Comparative Psychology of Mental Development.* New York: International Universities Press, 1948.

42. White, Jerome D., and White, Terri. *Self-Fulfilling Prophecies in the Inner City.* Chicago: Illinois Institute of Applied Psychology, 1970.

43. Wyckoff, Hogie. "Women's Scripts." *Transactional Analysis Journal* 1, 3 (July 1971).

44. Zechnich, Robert. Personal communication. 1969.

Index

6 for success from BALLANTINE BOOKS Help yourself.

16   NE-5